Cursed

Braiswick

Once again I have to thank the *'MiS–FiT'* Cable Guy (also known as *'Alien'*) for his professional proof reading and manuscript editing skills, Dominic Edmunds for another *'crazy'* cover design, and all you Mackems out there, that I've met, talked too, had run-ins with, or become friends with. The experience gained from meeting you all, reading your *'bullshit'* on the World Wide Web, and following by far the greatest team the world has ever seen – SUNDERLAND AFC – has inspired me once more produce yet another book of bitter and twisted tales.

Cursed

P.D.Han

Braiswick
61 Gainsborough Road, Felixstowe, Suffolk IP11 7HS

ISBN 1898030057

Copyright © 2004 **P.D.Han**

www.author.co.uk/han

November 2004

Cover design by Dominic Edmunds

Printed in Kent
by JRDigital Print Services Ltd

Braiswick is an imprint of Author Publishing Ltd

Recap

The following tale relates to one man and his hobby, or that could be one man and his obsession. Either way what we have here is a story of love, of dedication, of passion, of glory, of hate, of vilification, of depression, all in all the continuing saga of following Sunderland AFC - by far the greatest team, the world has ever seen - as unleashed in the book Why Do I Do It? Cursed was spawned out of a number of unanswered questions from Why Do I Do It? Cursed also follows directly on from Why Do I Do It? exploring the mind of a Mackem who by chance or by mistake helped to start the Internet revolution with respect to supporting SAFC online; an Internet geek who created www.readytogo.net - one of the biggest independent web based football fanzines in the UK, which at its peak surpassed the official SAFC website in terms of daily visitors (supporters locally, nationally, and internationally by those who have an undying love for The Lads in red and white).

Why Do I Do It? started with Sunderland's relegation in 1997 and ended with Sunderland's relegation in 2003. In between, the fables spun are ones of passion, sadness, the obsessive nature behind the creation of the online SAFC community, the daily postings on the so-called 'infamous' Sunderland Message Board (the SMB), the banter, the cyber-violence, the secrets (though not all secrets have been mentioned - wink, wink) the ridicule of the Mags, and of course the reality of following SAFC both on and off the pitch.

Sunderland's relegation from the Premiership in 2003 resulted in a quite astonishing 2003-2004 season, and as the author of Why Do I Do It? discovered, cultivated many new 'adventures'. As such, the footballing literacy world begged for more. OK that was a lie, probably most people thought "oh no not another book of self-indulgent crap".

Well maybe it is, maybe it isn't, but contained within these pages is the continuing journey, one that looks back at Why Do I Do It? and how it became a local best seller, one that looks at the 2003–2004 season – the league, the cup run, the play–offs, the whole shooting match.

Therefore, what follows are stories of death, of anger, of hooligan confrontation, of vanity, of self–promotion, of the dark side of the Internet, of the decision to call it a day (well maybe). Cursed is a book relaying one man's affliction, the trials and tribulations of loving Sunderland AFC, a team often plagued with being perennial chokers.

Enjoy!

P.D.H

I

"A Mackem is for life, not just the Premiership!"

I sprint as fast as my tired legs will allow. My breathing is deep, my heart is pounding; my lungs feel as if they're about to burst. The sweat dripping from my forehead is intense but I cannot allow it to affect my vision as I push harder and harder moving ever forward in my quest. Obstacles lie ahead and I quickly start skipping to the left, then to the right, and then to the left again. Majestically I turn. Gracefully I slip past one hurdle and glide by another. I stumble slightly but somehow I manage to keep my balance. Composure, I must keep my composure. The end is in sight. I look up; my brain sends electrical impulses down through my body. A decision has been made and I pull the trigger as screams of *'shoot'* are yelled from afar.

Then I stop. Time stops. Silence reigns.

I hear only my heartbeat as it thumps, thumps, thumps. Motionless, I stare, watching my bullet, my shot thundering forward. And it is a perfect shot. It is deadly, it is without remorse. It is a killer blow. Then a roar unlike any other I've heard explodes as my bullet finds its target with pinpoint accuracy. Slowly I turn around. A middle aged balding man walks towards me. He raises a hand towards his mouth, and blows into a small silver looking object. A deafening high pitched whistling sound erupts as a dozen or more people surround me, kissing me, jumping on me. Their weight is too much. I fall to the ground but I am not frightened for they are my colleagues, my fellow warriors; seasoned soldiers who have fought hard, who have battled endlessly and now are celebrating the end of the war. My body is shaking, I feel faint and yet I'm filled with an overwhelming sense of euphoria.

Eventually I stand and walk back towards what is my starting position. Within seconds however the high pitched whistling sound pierces my ear once more and it's all over. Victory!

F. A. Cup Final
Sunderland 1, Newcastle United 0
Han (90)

I look up to the heavens. I'm smiling. I'm crying. The clear sky turns from blue to white and I'm confused as it hurts my eyes. I rub them and suddenly I find myself sitting up in bed. That whistling noise is repetitively hurting my lobes. It's my alarm clock! It's 7.00am. Reality returns, the fantasy ebbs away. It was all a dream. I sigh as I get up. If only, I think to myself, if only. Yeah right, me scoring a winning goal for Sunderland AFC in the F. A. Cup final! Then again I've probably got more chance of actually doing that than Sunderland has of appearing in any cup final these days. In fact there's probably more chance of me ending this book with *"I love Alan Shearer"* than there is of Sunderland having any decent cup run never mind reaching a bloody final.

It's Monday morning, May 12th 2003, the day after SAFC's *'last'* ever game in the Premiership (another defeat – the final insult being a crushing loss at home against Arsenal though to be honest it was on the cards and therefore not too much of a surprise), but for how long? The season is over; it's been the worst one ever in living memory; the humiliation I feel being a Sunderland supporter is still fresh; it won't go away, nor I feel, will it ever. What happened cannot be changed. It cannot be erased from history and unfortunately I feel that we will all have to suffer constant jibes from the black and white bastards up the road who won't allow us to forget this relegation either. Such is life – the ups and downs of supporting Sunderland AFC and the end of an era for me personally.

The dream is over, no not the one I've just had where I score the winning – and only goal – in the F. A. Cup Final against Newcastle United. No, the dream of supporting my team, the passion, the optimism, the dedication, the loyalty, the compulsive undying love has now dwindled to a mere interest.

2

I guess my life has become so complex over recent years that I've moved on; I've elevated myself to another plane of existence, one where Sunderland AFC 24/7 does not exist. The support is still there, the fire is burning, though it's now a flickering flame and no longer a raging inferno.

I've got a lot of blame to pass around, I can point the finger, or two at the Club, at those who threatened legal action against me, at those who promised so much but delivered so little. Mix that with all the other unwanted complications in my meagre existence and it becomes pretty obvious that I need some sort of sabbatical away from it all. I need to turn my back and walk away. Forever? Maybe, maybe not. Time will tell, after all time heals all wounds as they say, so maybe come August my own lacerations will have healed sufficiently to warrant a return to the Stadium of Light, take up my position once more and support The Lads as they push for promotion in the unwanted position of being stuck in Division One.

So, why do I do it?

Or maybe I should rephrase that *"why did I do it?"*

But is that why in terms of supporting or why in terms of walking away? Or is that why did I write "Why Do I Do It?" in the first place?

I decide that I must try my best to put behind me all the traumas that have encompassed me and look forward to a summer of rest and relaxation. However I had partially made my mind up that renewing my season ticket was not an option, mainly due to cost rather than taking up a stance of protest.

Also I have to point out that my wife had finally persuaded me to get a puppy, something she'd been nagging over for months, so much so that I'd eventually given in to her whines. As such any season ticket money I had pulled together was spent on a cute little puppy dog! It also meant I had something else to focus on pretty much straight away – the training of a little *'baby'* not to piss and shit all over the house. I could also get out for long walks where I could be alone with just my thoughts in my attempts to remove the curse of being a bitter and twisted basket case. It was time to forget about SAFC for a while, and time to turn away from the Internet and the burden

3

that Ready To Go had become. Strangely enough that element was pretty easy to achieve. RTG had, in my own humble opinion, slowly turned into nothing more than a glorified message board, a forum and just a forum for the wandering red and white cyber squatters to communicate with each other. I found that I had little time and more or less zero interest in updating this web site. It had thankfully evolved into being quite self-sufficient and as a result I could sit back and let it maintain itself adding the odd comment or report if, and that's a big 'if', I felt like it. The ease at which I could give this part of my life the cold-shoulder meant I had ample time on my hands to concentrate on other things – like writing this bloody book – in-between cleaning up the mess made by 'Anton' the cocker spaniel.

Apparently I went on a bit in 'Why do I Do It?' about ginger people, so much so that some have accused me of being prejudiced. Well you could say Anton the cocker spaniel being ginger (and white) thwarts any preconceived notion about me being prejudiced. Sorry, I felt the need to stress that point to shut up all those conspiracy theorists out there who hold up the 'you're being unashamedly detrimental' card. I'm not, so there!

Now you may be wondering why I chose the name Anton, and from a red and white perspective think it was chosen because of former player Anton Rogan. No? Oh, well I guess I'll move on then. Hang on though, this is my book and I'm writing this, so I'm going to tell you why the puppy was called Anton and it wasn't after a former player from long ago, who in my opinion, was shite. You see I admire the philosophy of Anton Szandor LaVey (the author of The Satanic Bible), though don't call me a Satanist. I am a Mackem, a pissed off one, but still a Mackem and I guess still proud to call myself a Mackem at that. I'm not going to dwell on religion and all the mumbo-jumbo associated with what is effectively a cult, but there have been times in my recent past where I often wondered if God actually existed. I look at myself in the mirror each day and apart from seeing an overweight ugly Internet geek, I see someone who for the past few years has had to put up with a helluva lot of shit constantly being thrown at him. The relegation of SAFC was just the tip of the iceberg as, below the surface, there was the injustice that I felt was handed out to me by the incumbents at the Stadium of Light.

On top of that the inability to cope with my parents' divorce, and my subsequent near self-destruction, enduring months of depression and paranoia made me question what I had done to deserve such punishment.

Why had my life been turned upside down?

If God existed, what had I done to upset him?

Had I been some sort of serial killer or Nazi SS General in a previous life, and so in this life was being made to suffer to make up for my past indiscretions?

I've been a law-abiding citizen all my life. I've never been arrested, never committed any law breaking offences, nor am I racist or fascist.

And yet for some reason all hell had broken loose in my head and all around me. It was as if everything and everyone I touched, or came into contact with, resulted in disaster.

Thus even though I'm not religious I started questioning issues of faith. Stumbling across The Satanic Bible and having analysed the book, once the fanciful and spellbinding rituals were ignored, I suddenly found a set of philosophical thinking that matched my own thoughts on life, the universe and why Sunderland Football Club appeared to be cursed.

Basically I'm a humanist. That's someone who isn't a *'true'* believer (I don't go to church), but isn't atheist either (though I do hope that there is some sort of after–life for if this is as good as it gets, well all I can say is *'for fucks sake'*), and although the *'dark'* side and the *'occult'* is an interesting subject, I'm no devil worshipper.

Well how can I be?

I'm a Mackem; it's those black and white agnostic infidels who are the satanic ones. My reading interests which stem around such cabbalistic doctrine is therefore the reason why the puppy was called *'Anton'*.

II

"We will never get relegated again – Bob Murray a.k.a. Mohammed Said Al–Sahaf!"

I tend not to reflect too much on the 2002/2003 season even if at the time of writing this it is still fresh in my mind. There's no point really. What's to reflect on that won't leave a bitter taste in your mouth or leave you foaming with anger and disgust? Relegation hurts at the best of times, but in this age it hits bad, and so much so that it can threaten the very existence of your beloved club. Relegation for Sunderland appeared to bring forth no end of reports and rumours about the Club going into administration due to mounting debts and lost revenue following their demise from the top flight.

As the summer months gained momentum the truth (well in my view very little) came out and SAFC appeared to be indeed in the shit. The alleged debt was huge and it meant selling practically everyone to anyone in a futile attempt to claw back enough money to survive and actually start a campaign for promotion. This also meant *'sacking'* (the official term is of course being made redundant, but come on it's just a polite way of saying you're sacked) around seventy to eighty *'ordinary'* employees, office staff, bar staff, turnstile staff, shop workers – you know the type of people I mean – those who earn just enough dough to survive, unlike the thirty grand a week salaries of some of the players.

Walking around The Bridges Shopping Centre and seeing the Club shop boarded up, closed for good was, a sad, sad site indeed. And more was to follow once the new season got underway. The number of shutters apparently *'permanently'* welded shut inside the stadium – the kiosks and the bars – was very depressing. Certain areas under the ground were now ominously desolate and morbid. Low crowds may be bad enough but to have half the ground locked up was a sombre sign of the times. It therefore prompted one obvious question as far as I was concerned. Who was to blame? Murray? Reidy? Fickling? Wilkinson? Flo? McAteer? Gray? McCarthy? But then again, did it matter any more? Whoever was to blame would never own up, and any attempt at trying to push the Club for an answer would only lead in my opinion to the usual deafening silence.

So with this particular chapter in Sunderland's illustrious history at an end we said goodbye to most of the first team squad; Sorensen, McCann, Thome, Reyna, Craddock, Gray, Phillips, Kilbane, Bellion, Medina, Macho, El Karkouri. Some of these departures were expected, some were sad, and others were a blessing. Kevin Phillips leaving was a big blow. We were parting with a legend, though unlike previous legends he pissed off a few supporters by remarks he made about wanting to move on, and by admitting that he was stale and had lost interest. Sunderland supporters expect 110% and nothing less in each and every game played. Players who are merely going through the motions thinking of the end of the season and the ease at which they can move on to another club lose a lot of respect. Phillips in my opinion fell into that category. He may be a legend, but he now falls shy of the loyalty factor that other legends showed – Rowell, Gabbiadini, and Goodman to name just a few. Kilbane leaving on the other hand was from my point of view a joyous moment to celebrate. Although he started the new campaign in Division One, come deadline day he was offloaded to Everton and for the first time in almost two years we could field eleven players! I'm sorry but I just didn't like him. He showed no consistency bar the shite variety and offered little option for attacking flair when on the pitch. He may have given his all each and every time he played, he may have defied the insults of the boo boys for almost two seasons by never giving in, but what can giving all of nothing achieve but nothing? He was also used by the Club in my humble opinion far too often as the players' spokesperson. Maybe this was an attempt to improve his popularity amongst the hard core of supporters who, to be blunt, hated him. It didn't wash. Half the time you simply wanted him to shut his trap, stop talking about commitment and getting it right on the training ground – he may have been the best thing since sliced bread in training, but when it came to what mattered most (playing) he was simply not good enough. I could go on and on about Kilbane, looking for positives, adding more and more put downs, but there's no point for I've made my point, and it's one that you're entitled to agree or disagree with.

Now out of the summer moves losing Jody Craddock was a real surprise especially as I saw McCarthy handing him the number five shirt (it was one of those things that stood out – the issuing of squad numbers and the top fifteen numbers being those who were obviously going to be in the starting line–up when the new season kicked–off) as a sign that Jody was part of the preferred defensive line–up for the promotion campaign. Money talks, however and when you're a club in serious debt the odd million here and there won't go amiss, even though the player(s) would (go amiss).

In hindsight it was a logical and economical move to sell players, especially the highly paid variety, to other clubs. It reduced the obscene wage bill, lessened the serious debt that SAFC were allegedly in and thus attempted to keep the sinking ship afloat.

Out of all the players that left, the lazy, inept, and mercenary arsehole known as David Bellion proved to be one of the best transfers in recent times – in terms of revenue – for Sunderland AFC. Kilbane may have been crap, but Bellion – Jesus. The kid thought he was talented and as a result grew a serious attitude problem. Loyalty was a word he Tippexed over in his dictionary. He wanted out and, from all accounts, arranged for his agent to stir it up and unleash rumours of poaching stories, finally getting a move to Manchester United. We signed him for nowt and via tribunal ripped off United for around two million quid (of course knowing our luck he'll probably turn out to be a superstar for the Red–Devils).

Trying to find something to smile about following relegation was a difficult task to engender. However I stumbled across the following which I did find mildly amusing albeit a rather ironic comment that appeared on the SMB (which if you are unaware is www.readytogo.net's online message board which means *'Sunderland Message Board'* and not *'Sad Mackem Bastards'*) titled *"Things You'll Never Hear At SAFC!"*

Kevin Phillips *"You know what? Right now, I couldn't hit a cow's arse with a banjo."*

Michael Gray *"I'm really not a very good captain. I think I'll get someone else to do the job."*

Phil Babb *"To be honest, I don't really have the ability to play in the Premiership."*

Sgt. Wilko *"I don't think I can keep this lot in the Premier League."*

Uncle Bob *"Here you go Howard, twenty million quid, now hurry – you've only got two days to spend it. There'll be another twenty million come June."*

Gavin McCann *"I don't really think Kevin [Kilbane] is very good. I spend my time covering for him. And as for Paul [Thirlwell] – for fucks sake."*

Peter Reid *"Sorry."*

The Cleaning Lady *"I'm off to polish the silverware."*

Emerson Thome *"Don't worry Kev, you just make the run and I'll put it on a plate for you."*

Kevin Kilbane *"It's so hard being the fans' favourite."*

David Bellion *"I'm Sunderland till I' die!"*

Stephen Wright *"I hate getting mobbed by gorgeous young ladies."*

9

SAFC *"Dear season ticket holder, as a gesture of our shame, please have 2003–2004 free of charge."*

The Fans *"Ah well, at least the Mags are doing well."*

The Fans *"I wish we'd stop this fancy passing stuff and just hoof it."*

For some unknown reason I have I the past always painted the Internet and to a certain extent the users of the SMB as being dark, miserable, and overall an angry mob to mix with, but there are occasionally some memorable jewels posted by the roaming hoards in cyberspace:

"Desperately trying to think of something to keep the spirits up, I thought of the games I've been to with my son. At most of them he's come up with stuff that gives me a wry smile and shows, once again, that kids can see right through adults. They include:

Spurs (away) *"Why are we booting the ball up to Niall Quinn when Niall Quinn isn't playing?"*

Arsenal (straight after Jody Craddock scored) *"Little baby Jake up in Heaven will be so pleased his Daddy scored."*

Speaking to Kevin Phillips *"If you like Sunderland as much as me and Daddy, you'll score next week when we need it most."* The following week he put us 2–1 ahead at Charlton.

Manchester United (to a typically overbearing Cockney Red on the train) *"Daddy and me support Sunderland because they're our team. We don't mind if they're bad. Do you support Man United when they're bad? Or just because they win things?"* The whole carriage cheered!

Chelsea (away) *"Daddy, is this a football ground or a shopping centre?"*

III

"If you don't like me then press Alt + F4!"

I'm going to sidetrack for a moment before getting back to football and the 2003–2004 season. When I wrote *'Why Do I Do It?'* I never thought for one moment just how popular it would become and how much publicity it'd generate – though not always positive. I wrote it, as I stated in it, as a means of therapy, reflecting on my life in general, never mind the support I have for SAFC, and of course the many wonderful adventures I've had in the realms of cyberspace.

Upon its release at the beginning of October 2003, it became an instant hit and was soon selling out fast online and offline. I therefore have to thank the likes of Martyn McFadden of ALS, George Forster at the SAFCSA, Steve & Dominic from Ottakars in Sunderland, Dave Chester from Hills Bookshop, and Viv from Ottakars in Darlington, all of whom jumped at the chance of stocking and selling the book, and hopefully they all made themselves a handsome profit. I guess I shouldn't have said that as it'll make people think I'm now *'git minted'* (to quote from a rather arrogant review of the book on Amazon's website). If I say I am minted though I will come across as being conceited – hey look at me I made loads of money (a bit like the holier than thou season ticket holders who would wave their semi–final tickets at those who did not renew their season tickets – nah, nah, nah, nah, nah, I've got a ticket you have not you sad fucks). If on the other hand I say I never made much money out of it nor wrote the book with profit in mind then certain quarters will say I'm lying. Basically either way I cannot win.

Moving on though, and from a publicity point of view, I must thank Simon Crabtree & Gary Rowell (Metro Radio), Simon Pryde (Radio Newcastle), Patrick Lavelle (The Sunderland Echo), and Jez Robinson (The Sunday Sun) for their unprecedented help in promoting the book, be it on air or in print. I am humbled and eternally grateful to you all.

However, for all the help and assistance I was given by the aforementioned people in promoting and selling *Why Do I Do It?*, there's always a downside and I always find myself confronted with unwanted obstacles – in this instance W H Smiths and their refusal to stock the book. I say *'refusal'* literally as I don't want to get caught out in terms of libel or for making derogatory remarks, but no matter how hard I tried to sell them my book, their somewhat clumsy and pathetic buying process resulted in constant rejection. Whereas Hills and Ottakars support local authors, W H Smiths demands you send off a copy of your book to their head office – which I did. I never got a reply and when I contacted them to chase up my query they couldn't find it, instead requesting I send them another copy. If you ask me some twat nicked it for himself. The second copy was sent and returned with a rejection letter (why I sent another copy is beyond me as it was never looked at – you can tell when a book has never been opened). And so W H Smiths no matter how much effort I or my publisher put into it wouldn't sell what turned out to be Sunderland's best selling local paperback for Christmas 2003. It does however stock books about Newcastle United, independently published ones like mine, written by fans, like me. Hmm. Does W H Smiths only deal with alleged media darlings? Some say the Mags are that (media darlings), but the truth of the matter is, they're scum and they know they are – is that the Mags or W H Smiths?

When I finally secured a deal to publish *Why Do I Do It?* (as I've previously said), I never thought for one moment how successful it would become. I'm not going to bullshit here but it was never going to be, nor was it intended to be, a financially rewarding enterprise. It was targeted at a very specific market and a local one at that. It did sell well, I did make a little bit of pocket money out of it, enough to pay off some debt – you know what I mean, paying off the credit card, well some of it, as well as paying for a buy now, pay later fridge freezer, which I didn't even have anymore!

Overall the book helped, even if I'm being vain here, to establish myself as an author. Well I enjoy writing, probably more so than updating the Ready To Go web site. I no have numerous projects planned – one of which is this sequel, a one year later addition to *Why Do I Do It?*

Why add to it you ask?

Am I not flogging a dead horse?

Well no, I don't think so. You see it makes sense to carry on where I left off. It also gives me the chance to thank again everyone who helped promote the book and to those who bought the book – assuming you liked it and it didn't turn out from your own perspective to be a pile of shite.

But enough of the vain, *"hey look at me I wrote a book, I'm great"*, which too many sad bastards will believe. *Why Do I Do It?* was a therapeutic exercise and if you have read it and read it properly you will understand that rather than as one Amazon review stated, an egotistical, self–indulgent, trumpet–blowing pile of poo which is funny as the review appeared on Amazon before the book was readily available to buy – the release date albeit October 1st 2003 was delayed due to some last minute changes causing a print delay, so work that one out! Ever judged a book by its cover? Someone must have and as ironically pointed out on the SMB:

> *Well, the book was so appalling I've not even bothered to buy or read it. And I'm a great one for reading books. Just the same angle as* 'the lads are so crap I don't even bother turning up. But I'm still a great fan me.'

It is quite amazing how many people wanted to shoot the book and me down upon its release, some of whom declared on the RTG web site that I had no right to advertise it. Like, duh, isn't this my site? Can I not plug my own piece of work that I'm quite proud of? Apparently not! Even when I was told it was the best selling paperback in Sunderland (haven't I already said that?) during the run up to Christmas (2003), someone who worked for Trading Standards wanted to know if what I was declaring was truthful. What the fuck was the matter with everyone? Was it some form of jealousy? Was it hatred of a fellow supporter? Had I written so much of bitterness that I had unknowingly made enemies? Or is that part and parcel of being a Mackem – everyone is cynical and pessimistic rather than being gracious and optimistic.

I could go on and on about the ups and downs, the battles won and lost in promoting my book, but if I do then I may actually fall into being somewhat egotistical and this chapter does indeed become a pile of trumpet blowing poo!

Anyway I'll finish off my Oscar thank you speech by thanking (again) you the readers who bought the book. Hopefully you enjoyed it. Well some of you did as I received a number of emails congratulating me on my success, many who felt as if they were looking in a mirror, such were the comparisons to their own lives and their own feelings regarding Sunderland AFC. A minority of people – mainly online – took it upon themselves to undermine the book at all costs. I have no idea why, but they were determined to state just how shite the book was, and how it "slagged off *all* SAFC supporters", and that basically it wasn't worth the paper it was printed on. The fact that they hadn't read it, hadn't seen it, nor knew anyone who had read it didn't matter. They were to all intense and purposes making a number of presumptuous remarks to say the least. I think it's called character assassination. In legal terms they could easily be done for defamation of character, but as they were probably little kids still wanking away to pictures of Britney Spears on their bedroom walls, pretending to be hard cases online when offline they are no more than spotty faced teenage geeks, I ignored their insults. It was, I suppose, publicity and when has there ever been such a thing as bad publicity? I will say though that for every one person who wanted to destroy me there was at least ten supporting me. And out of those who did read it a number queried why I hadn't mentioned certain things – issues I left out that had taken place on the pitch, off the pitch, and online. The truth of the matter is I either forgot to or just didn't have room to put them all in. Besides polishing off the book at the end of the season – where relegation makes your motivation for completing harder to achieve – to the point of being on sale in October may appear to be a long time, but when you've got a full time job, kids to entertain, a shopaholic wife and a dog that needs exercising, you have little time to sit down and compose.

But for the benefit of those who wondered about 'this' and wondered about 'that', here is a summary of what I think I missed out last time around. On the pitch I didn't mention the absurd case of mistaken identity regarding Milton Nunez and how SAFC was allegedly ripped off thinking they were buying a top class player who apparently was merely a lower league player. I also neglected to mention the departure of the likes of Danny Dichio, Andy Melville, Lillian Laslandes – I don't think I mentioned him at all, Patrick Mboma, and Bernt Haas. I never dwelt too much on Jody Craddock's baby son dying nor his love of painting and his interesting collection of art. Likewise I never dwelled on The Academy Of Light, the spiralling costs and lack of interest in general by many, both fans and the media. Online I reluctantly left out the fact that as well as Gary Rowell being part of the backroom staff, for a short while so was Craig Russell. I also managed to contact Barry Venison who initially agreed to join RTG and write occasionally for us, but backed out at the last minute, as due to his colourful playing career he didn't want to associate himself to one particular former club. For example if he wrote for us and Liverpool FC's version of RTG got in touch, then wouldn't be able to commit to write for both so he said it would be better to write for neither. Fair enough. Yet a few months later he was a regular columnist for Kop Talk – the Liverpool version of RTG! Is Mr. Venison therefore two-faced? Is he embarrassed about being a Mackem? Or maybe the fact that he signed for the Scum made him somewhat nervous about re-associating himself with us red and whites?

I also carelessly overlooked Ready To Go's one and only attempt at raising money (for a good cause), something which was promoted via an online strip tease to win a signed strip – the winning donation going to Breast Cancer Care. Actually I'll mention a few things about this. The online strip tease came about due to an idea of get a sexy looking blonde to strip naked and therefore produce a set of pictures showing this bird in varying stages of undress (undressing fully clothed from a SAFC strip). A friend of my wife had suffered from breast cancer and with her husband being a keen amateur photographer, it didn't take long to put the idea into practice. I've no idea who the blonde was – my wife's friend sorted that one out, but to strip off in front of complete strangers during the photo shoot was a brave and admirable thing to so – a good egg all round. The photos were scanned and converted to use on the web site and with a little help from Photoshop's smart–blur filter, the quality of images – if you know what I'm talking about – was *'enhanced'*. With the *'prize'* being a signed shirt it meant that I had to run the gauntlet of autograph hunters prior to the next home game thrusting a replica shirt and marker pen in the faces of the players, though shame on Kevin Kilbane, Kevin Philips, Alex Rae, Gavin McCann, and Mickey Gray for snubbing not just me, but the kids who desperately wanted their idols to sign their shirts or caps or programmes. They were brushed aside as if there weren't there. Too big for their boots? Had they forgotten that the fans made them what they were and paid their obscene wages? By all means ignore me, an adult, but not the kids (I still managed to get all the players' signatures eventually though – Simon Crabtree sorted that one out for me). In the end the exercise raised over £300 for Breast Cancer Care and thus I felt a warming sense of achievement for doing something that when I look back on, I'm quite proud of.

Other than this I suppose I need to mention RTG's renowned anti–Mag baiting sections that was *'severely'* unleashed on the Internet community. A failed resurrection of my old FTM Executive Club was cut short in its prime, mainly due to lack of interest, but upon its re–launch was greeted with applause. The online strip tease resided here as did a comic strip invented by a mysterious entity known only as *'Smoker'*. He created an animated cartoon called *'The Wanker's Hat'* – about some wannabe player called *'Alan Wanker'* (who wore a wanker's hat and played for Scum United for he was a fucking twat). This monthly comic strip followed the fortunes of a boring lad from Tyneside who rose to infamy via an apprenticeship with Southampton – though initially he had issues registering to become a professional, as apparently he had no birth certificate! Alas this sad individual won a championship medal with Blackburn Rovers and before fucking off to Tyneside celebrated by mowing the lawn and creosoting the fence in his back garden. In true Viz style here was something with a black and white twist to enjoy and laugh at – and in my opinion better than the toilet humour served up reading *'The Fat Slags'* or *'Roger Melly'*.

This wonderfully cultured piece of anti–Mag propaganda was complimented with a collection of a few thousand *'Geordie'* jokes. For example:

> *On the sixth day God turned to the Archangel Gabriel and said,* 'Today I am going to create a place called Sunderland. It will be a land of outstanding natural beauty. It shall have a sparkling sea with an abundance of sea life, and wonderful sandy beaches.'
>
> *God continued,* 'I shall make the inhabitants prosper, I shall call these inhabitants Mackems, and they shall be known as the friendliest people on the earth. Their beer shall be as nectar, their women beautiful, and their football team, the greatest in the land, inspiring hitherto unknown passion and loyalty from their supporters.'
>
> 'But Lord,' *asked Gabriel* 'Don't you think you are being JUST A BIT too generous to these Mackems?' *At this, God started laughing fit to bust* 'Not really,' *he said* 'Just wait and see the neighbours I'm going to give them.'

A Geordie family were shopping in the Metro centre, and ended up in a sport shop. Little Billy suddenly puts on a Sunderland shirt and says to his sister, 'Look, I'm a Mackem!' His sister slaps him across the face and orders him to show their mam. He wanders over to his mam and says, 'Mam, look, I'm a Mackem.' His mother also slaps him across the face, and orders him to show his dad. He finds his dad and says, 'Dad, Dad, I'm a Mackem.' His dad looks at him and them he also slaps him across the face. On their way home in the car, the family turn to him and say, 'Well we hope you've learned something today' to which Little Billy replies, 'Yeah, I've only been a Mackem for two minutes and I already hate you Geordie twats!'

Newcastle is apparently under investigation by the Inland Revenue for tax evasion; they've been claiming for Silver Polish for the past twenty years.

Did you hear that the Post Office has had to recall their latest stamps? They had pictures of Newcastle players on them. People couldn't figure out which side to spit on.

There were two fat Geordies in a bar. One says to the other 'Your round.' The other says, 'So are you, you fat bastard.'

And of course I mustn't forget the FTM Awards, RTG's very own version of those silly Darwin Awards looking at unfortunate and tragic (but also humorous) deaths, our version aimed at the Geordies. For example:

During a post match party at a farmhouse somewhere North of the Tyne, a certain Geordie staked a strong claim to being the most macho man 'alive' by cutting off his own head. This unnamed person had been drinking with friends when it was suggested they strip naked and play some 'men's games'– stripping naked apart from their beloved black and white tops that is.

Initially they hit each other over the head with cans of Newcastle Brown Ale, and then smashed bottles of Brown Ale over each other, but then one man seized a chainsaw from the workshop at the back of the farm and cut off one of his fingers. To go one better another decided to cut off the end of his foot.

Not to be outdone, our main character in this grabbed the saw and crying 'Watch this then!' *swung at his own head and chopped it off.* 'It's funny,' *said one of his friends later,* 'Cos when he was young he put on his sister's underwear. But he died like a man.' *A tragic story, which prompts the question, do all Geordie men wear women's underwear?*

A Geordie left nothing to chance when he decided to commit suicide. He stood at the top of a tall cliff and tied a noose around his neck. He tied the other end of the rope to a large rock. He drank some poison and set fire to his clothes. He even tried to shoot himself at the last moment. He jumped and fired the pistol. The bullet missed him completely and cut through the rope above him. Free of the threat of hanging, he plunged into the sea. The sudden dunking extinguished the flames and made him vomit the poison. He was dragged out of the water by a kind fisherman and was taken to the hospital, where he died of hypothermia.

There's a lot more I could talk about but unfortunately there just isn't enough room. Maybe another time, eh? I must however finish this chapter by thanking the many varied and objective feature writers that have graced the pages of RTG over the years, *'The Yankee Mackem', 'The Oriental Mackem', 'The Singapore Mackem', 'The Oz Mackem', 'Mackem X', 'The Cockney Mackem', 'Alien*FTM*', 'The Mackem Angels', 'The Hampshire Mackem', 'Winston O'Boogie', 'Bobby Zimmerframe', 'Walter The Dog', 'The Smogmonster', 'The Quaker', 'The Monkey Hanger', 'Chris Liddle', 'Keith S30S', 'Streaker,'* and *'Tsunami'.* And now, back to footballing matters.

IV

*"There is a reason why there's only red
and white blood cells, it's in the blood!"*

When the new campaign (2003–2004) got under way, the general feeling amongst many was still that of anger and bitterness towards the previous terms farcical display. A comment I came across on the SMB, which was from a football web site that I have to admit I cannot recall, stated:

> *"Can you really name any Sunderland player worthy of an accolade of any sort this season? Imagine their Player of the Year awards! Sunderland is officially, and by some margin, the worst team in the history of the Premiership. Phil Babb was tipped as the man to watch, and although he was initially a fixture in the side he was dropped in mid–February and did not play under the Club's third boss of the season, Mick 'played nine, lost nine, scored two, conceded eighteen' McCarthy. "*

That said a lot really, but this is Sunderland AFC, remember. This is a club of tortuous virtue. We are cursed to fail whenever any golden opportunity arises. And when there is no opportunity, there is little hope of joy. Well there is some joy. Every now and then we are on top of the world and everything is rosy. But when things go pear-shaped they do so in biblical proportions and that hurts us all. The pain is colossal. We are Sunderland fans and that means we are often crucified for our sins. And our sins amount to no more than our love of the Club. We experience emotions beyond reason and rational. After all, how many supporters of other teams can have such a wide margin of emotional experience in recent times like:

- Worse team in the history of the Premiership!
- Nineteen points.
- Three managers in a single season.
- A hat trick of own goals by one of our own in a comedy performance Laurel & Hardy would've been proud of.
- Thirty-two shots to nil (Liverpool away)
- The 1998 play-off game considered by many as the greatest game of football ever seen at Wembley since England won the World Cup.
- All those incredible last day relegations.
- Cheating opponents especially Coventry City who twice managed to manipulate kick-off times to ensure our results were known, thus giving them an unfair advantage.
- 1973.
- The Bank of England Club.
- One-hundred and five points and ninety-seven goals in a season.
- Three defeats in forty-six games.
- Losing play-off finalists who still get promoted.
- Fans who remain calm, collective, and admirable during scenes of some of the worse soccer related violence in the past two decades (Chelsea away - Milk Cup semi-final), Newcastle away (Play Off semi finals).

Relegation had come once more to plague the city. But that was now history and there was nothing that I or anyone else could do to erase the nightmare. Sunderland AFC - by far the world's most extreme roller coaster ride.

Fast forward. The new season was here and time for a change in fortune - right? Wrong for there was to be a few more items to add to the extremity list and to begin with, we lost the first two games away to Forest and home to Millwall. The home game produced an inept display and an inept crowd.

The Stadium of Light was half empty or half full depending upon your point of view. It showed that antipathy and to an extent, hostility still existed. Enough was enough for far too many. They had deserted a sunken ship a long, long time ago and would not return until some sort of improvement was made.

An away game against Preston North End approached and as a result a media frenzy took place as Sunderland looked to avoid not just another defeat, but, as a consequence of losing, they would be tarnished with a record matching that of Darwin FC, a non–league outfit whose eighteen in a row league defeats was a record that they had held for some 105 years. Apparently they did not want to lose that record and I don't think any Sunderland supporter wanted to take the record from them either.

The match generated immense publicity, more than it would have normally and as a result something must have clicked with the squad, boosted by the support of Darwin who had raced to the game following a match of their own (which they lost) to cheer on the Lads.

Sunderland won 2–0 thanks to goals from Marcus Stewart and Sean Thornton. It was a turning point. We won the next three in a row and jumped into an early play–off position in the league (the pick of the bunch for me being the 2–1 home win over Crystal Palace and a last gasp injury time winning penalty from Marcus Stewart – talk about tension).

Maybe we could do a 'Leicester' and not a dreaded 'Sheffield Wednesday' after all.

We then started a run of ridiculous inconsistency losing away to Stoke before drawing away to Derby, the equaliser coming in injury time from goalkeeper Mart Poom. The ex–Derby player raced to join in with a Sunderland last second, last ditch corner, rising majestically and towering above everyone else in a packed penalty box. Unmarked, he powered a header into the top corner.

In similar vein to Tommy Sorensen's penalty save against Alan Shearer, Poom was instantly tagged with the status of 'legend' and so 'The Poominator' was born. It was a defining moment, more so when local brewers Darwin Breweries created Poominator Ale to commemorate the goal!

The bizarreness of that game generated a buzz of excitement, and with an *'easy'* midweek home tie against third division Huddersfield Town in the League Cup, a sense of moving forward was rapidly felt by all.

Alas we crumbled and lost 4–2. If promotion was to occur it wasn't going to be a walk in the park. Even though this was the League Cup, the irregularity was ever-present. The ability to fall apart like this would also mean in my opinion a one off season in the Premiership should promotion be re-achieved.

The squad was just not good enough. If we went up, we'd have to spend to survive, but we were a club close to administration from all accounts, so that was something you just couldn't see occurring if such a scenario ever arose.

Conjecture and speculation.

Contemplation and deliberation.

Postulation and cogitation.

Sunderland supporters now more than ever were going through a varied range of emotional meditation and theory, one minute promotion is on the cards, the next it's the play offs, and at times nowt. But either way it signalled more positive vibes than negative ones.

V

"When anyone is replying to a matter before he hears it; that is foolishness on his part."

Apparently there's no hiding place on the Internet for those in the limelight, such is its openness, its capacity to allow the surfer to be anonymous and thus spread gossip and rumours like wildfire with little or no ability to be traced. Message boards are the ideal breeding ground for those wanting to tell it all, or originate certain events, which if posted in an astute manner can easily be picked up and forwarded on via other forums or via email and at times faster than a virus can spread.

For example, in September 2003, around eight Premiership footballers were accused of gang–raping a seventeen–year–old girl in a Park Lane hotel (it seems there's a Park Lane in London too). Normally alleged rapists are not identified especially to the media until they have been formally charged. However when you're talking about footballers then the potential for the names to be mentioned, especially via the World Wide Web is more than likely.

Following the news of this shocking tale, the hunt was on to identify who the players were. You see it makes great terrace banter should they belong to your rivals or worse still anger and outrage if they belong to your own club. As it took place on a Saturday night on one particular weekend, and with those involved being purported Premiership stars, the identity as to which teams they belonged to was narrowed down to less than a handful. Speculation was indeed rife.

The lawyers of the suspected players started to furtively roam cyberspace looking for any site that mentioned their clients by name, and thus ensuring a guaranteed case for libel. A number of hooligan or right–wing related forums had either deliberately or unwittingly posted the names of the players allegedly incriminated and as a consequence a large percentage of these sites were suddenly and without warning closed down, either temporarily or in some cases permanently.

The SMB was an ideal target for the shifty whistleblowers to post names as speculation regarding the rape was rumoured to involve players from Newcastle United who had played Arsenal on the previous evening.

A suspicious sudden increase in the number of new registrations to the SMB became alarmingly evident, as new and obviously unscrupulous people were intent on naming names. However should a libel case be sought, it would be served on me, and my partner, as owners of the SMB, and not the anonymous arseholes thinking they were clever by telling it all. We had little choice but to tighten up and stop all new registrations and delete any post no matter how obscure which hinted at the possibility of libel. I'd been there before because of the actions of unknown entities – the hallway(s) that to all intents and purposes fucked me up and almost cost me my hobby, my job, my house, and my day-to-day livelihood.

A warning was posted that instant and permanent access to our message board would be removed and instigated without notice should anyone push the boundaries and threaten the existence of RTG, the SMB, and my own sanity, after all message boards were closing left, right, and centre, large and small, independent and corporate, unknown and well known. Should the allegations be true then any mentioning of names or so-called events that had taken place could mean that any subsequent arrests and convictions could be quashed in the courts.

Look what happened with the high profile collapse of the first trial of then Leeds United players Jonathan Woodgate and Lee Bowyer after the Sunday Mirror printed an allegedly prejudicial article.

For some reason we had a battle on our hands not only from the new breed of half-witted imbeciles intent on causing havoc, but regulars who couldn't or wouldn't accept our *'if in doubt, delete it'* rule. I'm sorry if you were caught up in all of this and upset by the zero tolerance that was instigated, but let me put it this way, who would go to court, who would be served some sort of injunction or legal action against them, you or me?

When the likes of Microsoft take a decision to close down all of its chat rooms in a move to clean up the web and the dangers associated with paedophiles, child pornography, kidnapping, and the likes, then deleting messages that mentioned certain players or teams was nothing that caused me stress or worry.

The thing is, the story was dominating not only UK web sites but also the national newspapers, radio, and television. People wanted to talk about it and to a certain extent there's nothing wrong with that. Some of the conversations on the SMB were clean, were thoughtful and interesting to read, but then along came a wanker to spoil the entire thread by declaring so

25

and so are the players involved, and that they were Mags and here's a chant for us all to ridicule them with.

Topic deleted!

Outcries of *'where's the thread gone'*, or *'there was nothing libellous in it last time I looked'*, was often declared. That may have been true, but since the last time they had looked someone had joined in with the debate and basically vandalised it. Thus it was removed, quickly, concisely, without thought, without remorse. The libellous posting continued however and so a good old cat and mouse chase ensued, deleting messages, banning people, warning people, posting messages asking for common sense to prevail which the vast majority adhered to; it was the minority of idiots who decided not to play ball.

Then just as the event in question died down and a level of prudence was restored, the players' names were made public knowledge and the whole scenario raised its ugly head once again. *'The player's names are now in the public domain'*, the SMB users would declare, *'so that makes it all right to mention who they are.'*

No it doesn't was my thought.

Regardless of whether they were or not, RTG wasn't in a position to defend any case brought forward by a lawyer representing a player compared with that of a national newspaper, or did the punters out there believe RTG was some sort of financially sound conglomerate?

Once again everything died down – for a while – but then Jody Morris of Leeds United was arrested for similar accusations and the game kicked off once more – a third quarter assault! This case was slightly different as the player involved was named rather quickly. Likewise the charges were dropped rather quickly too.

This whole saga proves my point though, about the Internet and the danger it poses to society in general. Anonymity allows anyone to act however they please, regardless of their normal real life behavioural patterns. Online they become evil – plain and simple. Hiding behind a keyboard, they act in a manner they would never dream of doing so in reality. It's a fetish, they get a kick out of it, a fix needed to satisfy their repulsive behaviour, the drug they inject into themselves to gratify their twisted and warped brains.

What's equally as sad is that these people are not, as you might expect, the degenerates of life. Many are highly paid people in highly respected jobs, with families and morals of a respectable nature. The Internet, though, is a method for them to jerk off, to be dirty, to get the adrenaline flowing and satisfy their dark fantasies regardless of subject matter – point in case Graham Coutts jailed for life in February 2004 for murder. The Internet was partially blamed for the killer's actions, as he was obsessed with Internet pornography and bizarre web sites showing images of strangulation.

So even though this book and chapter refers to football, one has to ask how far is far enough when it comes to obsessive and macabre behaviour on the World Wide Web?

How many people out there use the Internet to satisfy their fantasies, be it pornography or violent cyber hooliganism. How many of these people's loved ones, friends, family, and employers are aware of their covert sinister activities?

Are you one of these sick individuals?

Have you got secrets locked away in your Internet cache and history folder?

Sooner of later you'll get caught out. It's a high price you'll pay, and one you'll probably deserve too.

VI

*"You foolish fool, you think you're so funny,
yet all you do is amuse yourself!"*

A run of three away games saw three differing outcomes that kept the consistently inconsistent run going. Gillingham away ended in a 3–1 victory, and although any away victory is sweet, against Gillingham – which is rare, though not down to having a bad run against them, but down to the fact that the two teams are hardly ever in the same division as each other – is always something special. We all remember being relegated to Division Three in 1987, having lost to Gillingham in the relegation play-offs that were in force back then. To make matters worse the two-legged tie ended six all on aggregate, Sunderland losing out to the dreaded away goals rule. Each and every time we play the Gills, memories of those games always come flooding back – well they do to me. I was just a bairn, but I remember standing on the Roker End watching the Lads give it their all. Shiney Bennett scoring a beauty, celebrating by just standing still to absorb the atmosphere and the emotions everyone felt inside Roker Park. We won 4-3 that day, but it wasn't enough. Hardly any Gillingham fans turned up for that match. Instead their away allocation was full of Mags, cheering on our demise. Is it any wonder we hate those black and bastards so much. Anyway this particular win was always going to be a tricky one. Games against sides like this are must-win games for any team seriously thinking about promotion. The following away game, against Crewe, was similar in vein. Although not exactly a bread and butter match, it's still a game when looking at the fixture list you'd forecast three points in the bag. I know football doesn't work like that, but it's how I believe we fans look at things. Annoyingly Crewe 'stuffed' us 3-0 and to be honest I found that result quite embarrassing. I know Sunderland don't have a God given right to win every game they play, nor should they expect to just turn up at places like Crewe Alexandra's cow-shed, garden shed, and/or tin shed Gresty Road and walk away with three simple points, but the defeat was not only a set back, but humiliating at that. It proved once more that getting back up at the first attempt would be anything but easy.

To finish off this away run of inconsistency we drew 1–1 at Highfield Road, Coventry, which to be honest isn't anything to be ashamed of. All teams will target away matches as ones to gain at least a point from. On top of this, if you can win all your home games, then the division will be handed to you on a plate. An otherwise dull Monday night Sky Sports broadcast hit the headlines due to the sickening injury sustained by SAFC midfielder Colin Healy. With around ten minutes remaining, Coventry midfielder Youseff Safri flew into Healy, tackling him so badly that even watching it on television you could hear the crack, and subsequent replays showed a horrific break that looked to be a career ending injury. To witness someone have the bone in the lower half of their leg snapped in half was excruciatingly nauseating to say the least. I can put up with Hollywood style *'slasher'* movies without a care in the world, but seeing something so sickening in reality is another thing altogether. Healy may not have been the greatest of players and had up to that point not shown the promise so many thought he would bring to Sunderland, but no matter how much you may perceive a player as being no more than average or no matter how much you may not like a player, personally speaking, I'd never wish any such injury upon them. It's a shame that opposition fans don't feel the same.

A Sky Blue website that *'prides'* itself on being the longest serving and most popular Coventry City Football Club website in existence (yes, apparently they've got more than one), decided to be blunt, rub it in, and basically vindicate and exonerate what had taken place.

Apparently this *'supporter'* hoped that Colin Healy's playing career would be over. It was payback as Sunderland, a bunch of *'cheating c*nts'* were 2–0 up on the career ending injury tackles made between the two clubs (one being a tackle made by Nicky Summerbee on Steve Froggatt a few seasons prior, the other escapes me at present).

Unfortunately I haven't reproduced word for word what was said for I doubted I'd get permission from this idiot to use his piece, even though it was so distasteful I see no reason why I should obtain permission. Hopefully the sad and venomous vendettas people online attempt to play out will cease at some point. People like this in my opinion need psychiatric help. Even I wouldn't stoop so low even if the likes of Alan Shearer suffered such an injury. In this example, however, the Sky Blues *'author'* doesn't stop with football.

As well as running his Coventry website he also runs a so-called *'satirical'* website breaking bad news or rather revelling in it. It appears that he is obsessed with death, war, murder, rape, anti–socialism, and whatever else in terms of daily news that we read, watch, or listen too that hits us hard and affects us all deeply.

This sad fuck's other site thought it would be good to put together an article about the Soham murders poking fun at Maxine Carr (which many will not disapprove of), but the gall he had in running a *'competition'* to win the Manchester United shirts that Jessica Chapman and Holly Wells had worn at the time of their disappearance was deplorable.

He even had the audacity to state that he was offering a chance to keep a little part of Holly and Jessica alive forever by running this competition to win their shirts once the police and forensic experts had finished with them!

Can you imagine if the parents of the girls had seen that? What type of sick and twisted individual would stoop so low as to run a website that prides itself on writing up articles like this?

Once again it's easy to hide behind words and behind a computer screen in order to shock, but the line has to be drawn somewhere. If you ask me, this person's computer needs seizing, as it may well be full of tasteless and illegal material. Whether or not the author of this *'competition'* was the same person who wrote the *'let's celebrate Healy's broken leg'* article is beside the point as the two websites are under the editorial control of the *'Hurrah for Safri'* author.

I'm sorry but as a father myself people who play on such tragedy need locking up in a straight jacket. I can't imagine for one minute that they have kids of their own.

To me they fit the profile of a loner, a stalker, and most definitely a parasite. By the way I hope you don't think I'm being two–faced here by referring to these articles.

My intention is not to glorify this person's immature and disgusting taste, but to point out and raise what to me is offensive, revolting, and pathetic.

VII

"You want some eh?"

Colin Healy's absence left a major dent in Sunderland's midfield as the number of injuries building up reached crisis level. Jason McAteer was becoming more and more injury prone. The early season form of Paul *'The Crab'* Thirlwell was cut short by injury and now fans' favourite Sean Thornton was injured. Called up as a stop–gap replacement was short–term arrangement Jeff Whitely, who by being given this golden opportunity to shine, and earn a long term contract jumped at the chance – and proved to be a bit of a revelation. Mick McCarthy's transfer *'wheeling and dealing'* was limited and restricted to loan players or free transfers – such was the alleged state of debt Sunderland was in. His signings so far however had been admirable to say the least. Gary Breen was to date player of the season. The departure of Jody Craddock had left a gaping hole in our defence, but Breen slotted in with ease, settling the back four, remodelled the defence, and filled whatever combination of fullbacks and central defenders playing around him with confidence. McCarthy's ability to reassign players into different roles was also paying dividends. Julio Arca was now left back and showing he had excellent defensive capabilities as well his usual incredible talent. George McCartney was now partnering Gary Breen at the heart of the defence and proving he could handle a centre half berth without any worries. Stephen Wright, a scapegoat from the previous season was now showing why we'd bought him as right back. Maybe Division One football was his level. Regardless though, he was handling his role as many had expected twelve months previously, and to his credit had notched up a goal (at home against Watford). Up front Kevin Kyle was, as far as many were concerned, taking over from where Niall Quinn left off. Kevin Kyle is no Niall Quinn. That sentence isn't meant to be detrimental. Kyle is a different kind of player and one that the supporters of Sunderland shouldn't expect to be someone he isn't. He's young, and he's hungry. He's still learning his trade, and proving to be a handful to the opposition. Likewise, he could on occasion score. His partner initially was Marcus Stewart, and a player I felt hadn't been given much of a chance during the relegation season. He soon showed why he had been bought by scoring regularly, and up until Christmas, any game he scored in, Sunderland won. He was also a wise player, could attack viciously when it was necessary to do so, could hold up the ball when it was required to do so, and provide pin point passing as and when it was needed. His only downside was possibly a lack of fitness. Stewart would fade badly towards the end of a game especially in the latter half of the season. On loan for a short while was Stuart Downing from Middlesbrough, a winger in the mould of Alan 'Magic' Johnston, but his stay was cut short due to Boro's own injury problems. To bolster the strike force, in came Tommy Smith – another loan arrangement – from Watford, a player who had put Sunderland out of the F. A. Cup the previous season in a game remembered for a farcical retaken penalty that Smith converted at the second attempt. Another striker brought in was Darren Byfield from Rotherham, a surprise transfer as it saw the swapping of Byfield for Michael Proctor, a youngster who promised so much but didn't deliver consistently enough to keep his place in the team. On his debut for Rotherham however he scored twice! The usual outcry certain elements of the fans have towards unknown transfers once again arose – *"Who the fuck is Darren Byfield?"* and *"Never heard of him!"* or *"Well he can't be that good if he's coming from Rotherham!"* You know sometimes we give new players no chance whatsoever. Remember when we signed someone called Kevin Phillips? At the time, did we give him a chance, did we not expect, or demand, a name? Did we not say, *"Who the fuck is Kevin Phillips?"* You'd have thought we'd have learned by now not to judge a book by its cover. Byfield soon silenced *'us'* with a debut goal of his own (though as we all know now he did not turn out to be a *'Kevin Phillips'*). McCarthy was in essence building a squad of strikers he could rotate at will. Fucking hell we were turning into Chelsea! Smith and Kyle, Kyle and Stewart, Stewart and Smith, Byfield and Kyle, Byfield and Smith, Byfield and Stewart – the possibilities were endless. However no matter how many strikers you have, without a decent midfield, and one that has vision to create rather than be defensive, scoring goals and thus winning games will not be a dead cert. Thornton's talent did help out in that department. John Oster on the wing provided an added element to Sunderland's attack and even though we weren't storming the division, we were slowly climbing into at least a guaranteed Play-Off berth. Players that were considered a waste of space, were now proving the boo-boys wrong, and although I don't consider myself a boo-boy, I too was being proved wrong.

Now unfortunately every team, no matter how successful they are, always have an element of the crowd who despise certain players, and with such hatred that they border on being racist, prejudiced, fascist, or some other anti-social disease that decent and respectful people find so despicable. Over the years a level of dissatisfaction has been vented out on certain players. Football fans, it would appear, need a scapegoat, someone to blame if and when things go pear-shaped. Think back over recent times and you can easily recall players such as Thomas Hauser, David Corner, Gordon Armstrong, David Kelly, Gareth Hall, Steve Berry, Dave Swindlehurst, Eric Gates, Paul Stewart, Kevin Kilbane, Bernt Haas, Peter Daniels – just a few of the players to don the red and white shirt only to have their ability or parenthood questioned by the boo-boy brigade, either occasionally or throughout their entire career with Sunderland. Existing players suffering the jibes were John Oster, Stephen Wright, Jason McAteer, Phil Babb, and Paul Thirlwell. I'll admit without admitting to any booing that the above list does contain players who were shite either throughout their career with SAFC or at some point in their career with SAFC! Some were still here and I'll come to that in a later chapter. However on this occasion even I had to take off my hat to the impressive improvement in form from the likes of Phil Babb and Stephen Wright. However some fans, regardless of form, appear intent on continuing to vent out their hatred towards certain players.

Sadly there is an element within the supporting ranks of SAFC that appears to be racist – their target, Jeff Whitely who of course is coloured. It is sad that any club, let alone Sunderland AFC, should have people who act so callously towards those whose skin colour is too dark for their own liking. However, despite what we are all told, racism is rife amongst society, always has been and always will be. Too many people still refer to the corner shop as the *'Pakki's'* or when fancying a take-a-way will head off to the *'Chinky's'*. We call the French *'Frogs'*, the Germans *'Krauts'*, the Mags *'Scum'*, Rangers call Celtic fans *'Fenians'*, blacks are *'niggers'*, Far Eastern people are called *'slanty-eyed'*, white people are *'trailer-trash'*, *'honkies'*, *'pigs'*, and *'ignorant fuckers'*. Sometimes we say things without meaning to be racist but are; other times we mean what we say. Look at Ron Atkinson, an established and respected former manager and television sports pundit, who off air with his microphone still switched on was caught calling Chelsea's Marcel Desailly, a nigger. Whether it was a case of being sacked instantly or whether he voluntary resigned, it was too late. In today's politically correct world, the damage was done, and no matter how many times he continues to apologise or vehemently state that he is not racist, what he said will haunt him for the rest of his life. That's how sensitive we are these days. No matter what background we come from, no matter what religion we may follow, or what colour our skin is, we all are or have been at some point in our lives racist.

To this day I still witness events that prove this *'hypothetical analysis'* of mine. I may even be guilty myself or may have been subjected to it by others. Rap music is just as popular these days as it was when it first became mainstream some twenty odd years ago. Yet no matter which artist's music we go out to buy and listen too, be it 50 Cent, Eminem, Tupac, Puff Daddy or P Diddy or Puffy or whatever he's calling himself these days, Snoop Dog, DMX, The Notorious BIG, Ice-T, Ice Cube (no not Vanilla Ice), the lyrics we listen too tell a tale of a rift in society and one that has existed for far too long. And yet hardly anything is done about it. They are just words in a song and we take it at face value rather than any statement of anger.

Away to Cardiff City we lost 4-1, but the defeat was unfortunately secondary to other elements of the game, namely sections of the Sunderland crowd chanting throughout a minute silence held for Wales legend John Charles and for a group wanting to send Jeff Whitely *'back to Africa'* – and that's a polite way of putting what they were saying. And yet hardly anything was done about it. Yes it was a minority. Yes the majority held their silence during the minutes mourning. Yes upon the referee's whistle the majority booed those who had disrespected football. But what does booing achieve in these situations?

If you want my opinion, fans should rally round reach other and kick the shit out of people who act like this. Racists, fascists and other elements that pride themselves on their anti-social behaviour and blatant prejudice aren't welcome in football and certainly not in the ranks of SAFC. I'm no racist, nor am I a hooligan, but I have to stick my neck out here and controversially say I admire those members of the alleged *'notorious'* Seaburn Casuals firm for twatting a couple of *'fans'* who had shown disrespect during the minutes silence at Ninian Park, and the unnecessary abuse thrown at Jeff Whitely. I think a few more of us should turn vigilante and give out justice onto those human scum who act as if we lived in the dark ages and not the twenty-first century. I guess the problem is, and I assume a problem with the law, is that by turning vigilante, we break the law, and it will be us who get punished and not the sad racist thugs. A thread that appeared on the SMB following Sunderland's home defeat against WBA discussed the issue of racism. This wasn't the first time such issues have been openly discussed nor will it be the last, but I felt the need to reproduce what was discussed here to show how people behave when it comes to a sensitive subject as this. The thread shows those annoyed by it, those who you could say condone it, and those trying to lighten it up a bit. The layout used indicates the nickname of the poster, who they support (it shows how sensitive subjects can bring together fans of other clubs to join forces) and what was said (grammar tidied up). There'll be a section on the type of topics that are created on Ready To Go's message board in a later chapter.

Subject: Racist Bastard In The West Stand

WIKI (Mackem): *Since my father died I often take my mam to the SOL, yesterday I wish I'd gone on my own. Approx. twenty minutes into the game this prick came out with "GET THE BLACK B*****D OFF". Now a few years ago I would most definitely have turned round and said something to him or report him.*

 When you do something like that you usually get a bit of verbal back and can become a bit heated and I'm afraid I wasn't going to subject my mam to any of that. So I turned round and looked at him just in the hope that he may rethink his next racist crap. You guessed it, no, to cut a long story short five more racist statements, each time I looked round to register my disgust, each time he saw me, finally backed by his three mates, he shouted "What you looking at" to which I again turned round just to let him know I wasn't happy with his verbal shite.

 After that, the racist crap stopped until Dyer broke away to cross the ball to Koumas and he shouted "KNACK THE BLACK C**T". I've tried to report this prick five times today on the hot line, each time it's engaged but I will get through, and I hope someone reading this either knows this gob–shite or actually heard him, if so report him too. Mind (although I doubt it) I do hope he reads this, I just hope he's at the Crewe or Norwich game, I'll be watching and waiting and I won't have my mam with me.

 I look forward to meeting you again you racist bastard.

SMATTY (Mackem): *Nice one. Scum like that, are not welcome.*

AIDC316 (Mackem): *You would think this matter would be taken seriously with the amount of effort the club invests in anti–racist programs. People of this mentality are just plain thick. The knob would have no doubt been singing the praises of Babb or Whitley had they scored a winner for us. Well done for taking a stance and lets hope he gets banned.*

BOB FLEMMING (Mackem): *Don't have a go mate you'll be the one who ends up in bother with the law. Keep persevering on the line and report this shit. Then, just hope Sunderland AFC do something about it. I know the powers that be would like to, just not enough done by the stewards.*

Well done for reporting it as well mate, many people, even though disgusted, would just let it pass.

MANCBLUE (Manchester City): *Fair play to you for having the balls and the decency to do something and make a stand. Sadly you can guarantee you will get the usual mindless fools replying, asking what is wrong with it and would you complain if they were shouting fat bastard etc. Hope you get somewhere with the complaint.*

PROJECT NIRVANA (Mackem): *I had a similar thing in the East Stand last year. Reported it to a steward who did nothing. Made a note of the guy's seat and the steward's number. At half time asked the steward supervisor for a quiet word; he was excellent and took me down to the concourse out of sight. Gave him the bloke's seat details and the steward's number.*

Nothing happened in the second half and the bloke continued but at the end of the match the bloke was pulled as he came down the concourse by the supervising steward with a policeman standing by. They chatted with him.

At the beginning of the next home game, the senior steward came and spoke to the bloke and told him that he was under CCTV surveillance. No problems for the rest of the season.

MACKEM DJ (Mackem): *Fucking Neanderthals. Do not stop in your efforts to report this twat, if it stays engaged, try another format, go straight to the club.*

NUMBER 2 IS GARETH HALL (Mackem): *Well done for reporting the twat. If you can't get through, perhaps see a steward at the next match?*

BILL (Mackem): *Complete disgrace shouting that at a footy game or anywhere else but I wonder if you would be saying this if he was shouting "Knack the ginger c**t".*

THE BANDIT (Mackem): *I'm not racist Bill, but that comment – tut, tut – you cretin.*

BILL (Mackem): *You're going to tell me what the fuck I said that was racist?*

WTDOG (Mackem): *While I can see Bill's obvious lack of common sense, this doesn't mean that the intolerant bastards can chuck their labels around with gay (and lesbian) abandon.*

THE BANDIT (Mackem): *I take it that's directed at me. I am chucking it round but certainly not with abandon. Why oh why can't big Bill have the balls to admit what he is instead of beating around the bush? At least then he wouldn't be a spineless fucker and have the courage of his convictions.*

WTDOG (Mackem): *I don't think that he will admit to being either a racist or a hooligan because it may be possible that he is neither. Both are emotive subjects. Both have defined sides. But there is still a middle ground.*

BILL (Mackem): *So you don't think it's stupid complaining about someone shouting about skin colour when it's acceptable to shout about hair colour? Just seems a bit stupid. And what is it that I am?*

THE BANDIT (Mackem): *Oh but he is, Wtdog. The worst possible kind – the snidey, won't admit it in public kind.*

BILL (Mackem): *You have never met me. You can not judge me just through a message board. I have never ever insulted people on their skin colour on this board or anywhere else and I have never said I have been involved in violence so you have no evidence at all.*

PROJECT NIRVANA (Mackem): *Clearly you know the difference. But just in case you don't, calling someone a "ginger c**t", of which I have no experience, but maybe you do, is just your bog standard simple vicious abuse. But to differentiate someone because of the colour of their skin is racism and as no doubt you know, as well as* *being a higher layer of vicious abuse and one could argue abuse of the worst type and sickening is also against the law. But of course you knew that didn't you?*

Bill said: "Yes I know that, I just think it's stupid that one is considered worse than the other".

Well based upon this comment you clearly don't know it despite your protestations otherwise which technically (at least) makes you a racist.

JONNY B (Mackem): *Just pinching myself to check that I'm not dreaming. Has anybody ever been murdered, exploited & beaten because of the colour of their hair?*

BILL (Mackem): *I apologise. I posted without thinking and posted a potentially offensive post.*

JARVIS (Mackem): *What's the hotline number mate? – I had a similar experience. Twat next to me at the same time (when Moore got injured) was the final straw – I confronted him (peacefully) and before I knew it he had grabbed me by the throat and was punching my head. It was over in about twenty seconds and to be honest I was much more pissed off about the racism than the assault and have sent a letter to the club today. Never known anything like it at the football before and if I get my way that bloke will never set foot in the SoL again.*

JOEMCDOKES (Mag): *Well he was black and he did set up the goal the c**t.*

TAFF (Mackem): *It's astonishing that we still have people on here that think discriminating against a person because of their skin colour is offensive. On a practical level, mate, my experience is that the best way to deal with this is to speak to a steward and give him the seat and row number although I hear that some are not interested, when we sat in the first row of the SW Corner next to the away fans, they were great. Email the Club. I've done this on three occasions and each time they acknowledge the email within a day and phone within a week.*
If you remember at the Coventry game this season there was a few choruses of "Yer just a town full of Pakis" and the Club took it real

serious. Please email them. After the Coventry game, the safety manager assured me that six season tickets were confiscated. Sorry Newcastle, but if these scum are in a NF march instead of a football game, they will be more closely supervised and we will have a better match day experience. And if Joemcdokes is kicked out of the SoL for good, we'll be none the worse. Idiot.

NUFCLAD (Mag): *It's called reading between the lines. Sounds to me like you are of the opinion that if it's ok to call someone a "ginger c**t", then it's ok to call someone a "black c**t". Well done Wilki, but don't get physically involved at all (or verbally) let the authorities deal with it.*

KNOBBY (Mackem): *Wilki, I was one of the people sitting next to you when this bloke started with the racial remarks. Can I point out that I have nothing to do with this man. He is not a friend nor would I associate myself with this type of person outside of the SOL. Unfortunately this individual has sat in that seat since the opening of the SOL.*

What he did was out of order and his remarks were well out of order. I hope you do get this individual removed from the SOL. However I do not wish to be associated with this person just because we have to sit next to them as that is my season ticket seat.

Neither I nor my friend are racists and we did try to stop this prat from hitting another individual who was sitting on the opposite side from him.

PETEB74 (Mackem): *Many moons ago I emailed the club about a Neanderthal bloke a few seats along from me making monkey noises (to Bruce Dyer when he played for Barnsley if I recall correctly).*

But I kind of took the coward's way out and sent it anonymously and said I was sat a few rows back. I've never seen the bloke again so I assume they took notice!

MATTYM09/109 (Mackem): *I look forward to the day I can call someone a black c**t the same way I call people a stupid twat for being stupid, a bald git for being bald and a knuckle–dragging ape for being a Geordie.*

The problem is we, as a nation, have done some mother fucking terrible things to people because of the colour of their skin. Things that nothing we do, no apologies, no constant enforced equality by liberals can atone for.

And worst of all there are still people out there that think less of people because of skin colour.

Or not even less.

Those whose heart rate rises, and they cross the street when they see a black guy, or worse a whole GROUP of them coming because "they know what that sort are like" are equally as culpable. Only when racism is dead, when no one behaves this way and idiocy of the past is finally consigned to the past will I be able to shout black c**t at a mate the same way he'd shout Mackem scum at me.

Unfortunately that time is not now as our past actions and the mindset of too many people still weigh down our entire society.

THE FLYING GRAYSONS (Mackem): *JonnyB asked if anybody had ever been murdered, exploited & beaten because of the colour of their hair. Well, lots of ginger Jocks have!*

GK (Mackem): *For their hair colour?*

THE FLYING GRAYSONS (Mackem): *Of course during the highland clearances they were identified by their gingerness, and wearing skirts as well of course.*

GK (Mackem): *But they weren't beaten for being ginger were they?*

THE FLYING GRAYSONS (Mackem): *No they were beaten, killed and driven from their home because of their race. They were identified by there racial characteristics (ginger) and ethnic dress exactly as most natives of other countries oppressed by the English over the centuries were. Or do you disagree?*

GK (Mackem): *They weren't beaten or killed because of their hair colour.*

THE FLYING GRAYSONS (Mackem): *No they were beaten, killed and driven from their home because of their race. They were*

41

identified by their racial characteristics (ginger) and ethnic dress exactly as most natives of other countries oppressed by the English over the centuries were.

Or do you disagree?

This could go on a long time. Why can't you accept that Caucasian people have been beaten and killed because of their race and those racial characteristics were used to identify the targets for the racist abuse?

GK (Mackem): *Because the beatings and killings you mention were carried out on Scots. They were beaten and killed for being Scottish.*

Jonnyb said: "Has anybody ever been murdered, exploited & beaten because of the colour of their hair?"

You said "Ginger Scots" *which is correct to an extent, but all other Scots with blonde, dark or purple hair were beaten and killed for good measure. Ginger English people escaped a beating. Anyhow, it's all irrelevant anyway.*

--NEMO-- (Mackem): *Very few were actually killed during the clearances. The majority were* "encouraged" *to leave for America by dumping them on the west coast without access to land or their livestock.*

THE FLYING GRAYSONS (Mackem): *Equally true for most races that had their land grabbed by the English. A minor point, and don't get me wrong on this, but it is a small victory that the language the racists use is being pushed back.* "Black bastard" *is offensive but there was a time when they could get away with* "black man", "monkey", "black man" *etc. It's why those monkey noises are so bloody annoying 'cos the gits can make them without being as easily identified.*

SYDNEY FAN (Mackem): *Can you two pull your heads in. This isn't a fucking court of law. He made a general reference and a valid point stating more than asking that no one had been killed for being Ginger. To which the common sense answer is no.*

However you have quoted an obscure irrelevant purge from god knows when to provide you with a technical yes answer. So both of you are right and for fucks sake let it go.

TOONTOON (Mag): *Grayson, you must be a ginger twat.*

THE FLYING GRAYSONS (Mackem): *That's Mr. Ginger Twat to you.*

TOONTOON (Mag): *He's ginger, kill the fucker.*

THE FLYING GRAYSONS (Mackem): *I'm Ginger and black!*

LANCHESTER RED AND WHITE (Mackem): *What, you Carlos Valderrama?*

[So how does one analyse and conclude this somewhat typical thread that will appear in numerous disguises on practically all popular football based Internet forums? Does one assume racism is still rife on the terraces, and do we also conclude that a genuine and serious topic fades into some failed attempt at humour which some will find amusing, but others won't – the underlying tone changing from pointing out racism to having a laugh – or being prejudiced towards the colour of people's hair? Where does one draw the line between humour and being offensive? This thread, it could be argued, started by discussing a serious problem existing with a certain type of 'fan' attending the Stadium of Light. The thread however moves on from its concerns over racism and onto a level of prejudice against people with red hair and in particular Scottish people with red hair. One can argue the shift in this thread was just a bit of harmless fun, but is it funny or will it upset people from Scotland who are redheaded? Are we being too sensitive these days? Has political correctness gone mad, or should we just look away from the seriousness of what's being said and look at the funny side of things? Whatever your own opinion is, I decided to put this in to show just how complex certain issues

43

are, and can be, and how the *'average'* football supporter will perceive such things by airing their views on the Internet.]

VIII

"Every day, thank the Lord that you are Mackem!"

Christmas always provides the football hungry fan with a feast of games over a short period of time. Normally for the Sunderland supporter it means guaranteed inconsistency and at least one embarrassment, point in case, Everton 5 Sunderland 0, 27th December 1999; Newcastle United 3 Sunderland 1, New Years Day 1985; Ipswich Town 5 Sunderland 0, 29th December 2001. It was therefore about time things changed and over Christmas 2003, SAFC played three and won three; Sunderland 2 Wimbledon 1, Sunderand 3 Bradford City 0, and Rotherham United 0 Sunderland 2. The points were indeed valuable considering we hadn't won since playing Gillingham away at the beginning of November. This fortuitous run continued however with a win over Hartlepool in the F. A. Cup followed by victory over Nottingham Forest putting us third in the league, six points off top spot. Fucking hell, were we actually going to bounce back at the first attempt?

The First Division really was a shite league in 2003–2004. Be honest, we weren't that good of a team. We struggled to score, struggled in midfield, lost games we shouldn't have, won games we shouldn't have, defeated some teams by the narrowest of margins, and lost to others shamefully. But such variations in results didn't fall solely on the shoulders of Sunderland AFC. Other teams were plagued by this inconsistency. Sheffield United, West Ham and Ipswich Town – three teams always forecasted as promotion contenders, and three teams who would put together decent runs only to suddenly fuck up. The only consistency belonged to the apparent runaway leaders Norwich City and relegation fodder Wimbledon.

Looking back at the game against the *'Wandering Wombles'*, a recorded seventeen Dons fans turned up at the Stadium of Light and you either have to laugh at them or admire them for their courage in supporting a team who have become a laughing stock in football. What I mean by this is how Wimbledon have uprooted themselves and moved to Milton Keynes. The way in which they've gone about trying to survive borders on the ridiculous and yet at the same time, can you blame them for not wanting to? Their fan base, it would appear however, has given up on them.

Milton Keynes appears not to be interested in them, point in case the game we played there in April, winning 2-1, sending the Dons into Division Two – half the crowd were Mackems (and coming two days after the F. A. Cup semi–final defeat shows the difference between fans supporting their club compared with those who just give up). I wonder though, how would we react if our Club uprooted and went off to play elsewhere?

Yes, Wimbledon fans should be used to it, for they had been squatting at Selhurst Park since leaving Plough Lane in 1991 due to the ground being too small and not meeting certain standards laid down by the Premier League.

I suppose the inevitable was bound to happen sooner or later, but once the announcement was made that the Dons were moving seventy miles north, the fans that had stuck by the Club's alleged temporary move to Crystal Palace fucked off.

In fact they formed their own club, AFC Wimbledon, generating crowds bigger than the Wimbledon club they had previously supported and although a non–league outfit at present, you have to admire the gall to make such a move, to turn your back on league football and start over.

AFC Wimbledon are now apparently three seasons – assuming promotion each time – from entry into the Third Division, and overall seven years away from potential Premiership football. It's a bit of a mess in my opinion and one that to be honest would never happen to Sunderland or any other club of such statue.

But what if it did happen, what then?

Would you continue to watch The Lads if they upped sticks and started playing in Berwick or Carlisle for example?

Or would you support a local non-league team? These questions were put to the users of the SMB, the answers varied;

"I'd support them wherever they went. I'd rather they were in Sunderland, but if a move would benefit them, then I'd stand by it."

"They already have and I already did. Or do you mean further than from Roker to Monkwearmouth?"

"No. If they moved to a different city I could not support them. I don't know what I'd do but I couldn't support another team either, not whole-heartedly."

"Can't imagine not supporting them. But let's face it, hypothetical question or not, it's just not going to happen."

"Well I feel sorry for Wimbledon. They need to change the name and start from scratch. They just aren't Wimbledon anymore."

"I'm glad I'm not a Wimbledon fan. It really wouldn't be the same. Part of the magic – especially as an exile – is the buzz you get from going home."

"No chance. Club and city are one and the same. If they moved to Washington or Seaham that would be tolerable since it's 'out of town' Sunderland but Berwick and Carlisle are totally different cities and the club would cease to be 'Sunderland AFC' and become the next 'Franchise FC'."

Wimbledon FC it would appear is doomed to failure. Milton Keynes hasn't taken to them, maybe the fact that they have been granted permission to call themselves Milton Keynes Dons FC will help, but surely Wimbledon's identity is now no more and although the AFC Wimbledon mob declare that they have kept the spirit and identity alive, they are not Wimbledon FC for they abandoned that club to start again.

Apparently there is a legal wrangling taking place over the rights to the history of the club, as AFC want historical facts such as F. A. Cup winners attached to the AFC version.

However it is the FC version that holds that record, but they are now called Milton Keynes Dons FC, so who has the rights to these records?

As you slowly start analysing the mess that this club is in the more you are grateful that your own club could never fall into such a quagmire.

Wimbledon FC/Milton Keynes Dons FC however are slowly dropping further down the league and appear to be heading towards non–league football faster than a Geordie on a Monday morning heading towards the local post office to collect his giro – and it is quite an achievement to beat that.

I think Milton Keynes sees this professional football club of theirs as a novelty. The fans that turn up do so wearing varied replica shirts ranging from Plymouth Argyle to Chelsea. The ground is being borrowed from the local council, and is to all intents and purposes an extension of a leisure centre complex.

Top this with the fact that the ground is more or less entirely open to the elements then on a night when John Kettley warns of torrential rain, the already low crowds just get lower and lower.

Part of me is saddened by the downfall of a club in this way, but this is Wimbledon were talking about, a team that defeated Sunderland 1-0 in 1997 and relegated us from the Premiership.

The 2–1 win Sunderland inflicted in April 2004 sent the Dons into Division Two, so I could say justice was served, or am I being too harsh?

IX

"We're going to need a bigger boat!"

I'm going to confess to being rather selfish now, as back in August, I received an email from Sky Television looking for a Sunderland Fan to take part in a mini series that was going to be filmed in London about the Premiership's greatest goals, games, players, etc. Basically they wanted one fan from every team that had ever played in the top flight to come on this show. The email asked if I would promote the event and direct people to vote for their favourite goal, game, player, moment, as well as nominating themselves to take part in the show. The words *'book promotion'* sprung to mind so I offered myself to Sky and just prompted the users of RTG to the voting side only. It meant that I was the only SAFC fan who put themselves forward to appear on the show. Annoyed? Sorry, but I saw myself on TV plugging my book, mixing it with the media, and the so-called celebrities that were also going to take part in order to spread the awareness of my North Eastern version of Nick Hornby's *'Fever Pitch'* further a field (yeah right).

However Sky or rather Maverick Television was filming the show on a Monday and all attendees had to be there prior to 9.00am. That meant getting to London from Sunderland would be an expensive and time-consuming journey, more so as Maverick wouldn't cover any travel or accommodation costs. The thought of promoting my book and selling shit loads was too big of an opportunity to miss out on so I thought I'd drive down on Sunday after contacting a close cousin of mine who just so happened to live in London. I was sure he would put me up for the night, especially seeing as he was now some sort of wannabe *'property tycoon'* buying up, doing up, and renting out houses left, right and centre, and as such would have plenty of room. I called him and the bastard said he was full up. I would've slept on the sofa but he said no. Twat. I thought we were close. I could've sworn you said anytime your down in London give me a call. Well thank you very much.

And so with no way of getting to London by 9.00am Monda morning and with no free digs to kip in, I got back to Maverick Television and told them I wouldn't be able to attend unless they'd help cover costs. My plans of world domination (in the literary sense) were put on hold. Of course by not promoting their request properly they never had any other nominees wanting to appear on the show, so they got back to me and said they'd arrange a hotel for me to stay in if I could get down to London on the Sunday. They wouldn't pay transport costs even though I was willing to drive down; they declined to pay for my petrol. So I said thanks but no thanks. Of course by not promoting their request properly they never had any other nominees wanting to appear on the show (didn't I just say that?), so they got back to me and offered to pay for me to go down by train, come back by train and put me up in a hotel for the night. On this occasion I accepted their offer. You see you never get anywhere in life if you don't take chances and try to keep the upper hand. I could've easily caved in and said I'd appear on the show and pay for everything myself. But come on, I'm a Mackem – we are renowned for being tight fisted gits.

One requirement from Maverick was that I had to make sure I took my colours with me but at the last minute I had to go out and buy a new top as I'd somehow put on quite a bit of weight in the summer. Yes, I ate all the pies and my replica top was too damn small. But nevertheless, packed with a change of clothes and a new replica shirt (though a retro one), I headed off to Durham railway station in anticipation of having my fifteen minutes of infamy.

Prior to the train arriving I noticed just how many 'Uni-Youths' were gathering on the platform. It became a bit of a circus and an interesting sight seeing how the future of our country behaved in public. As if suffering from some inferiority complex they would gather in small packs of about four or five and begin a ritual of talking loud about their studies, their political analysis of world events – as if we give a fuck. This weird mating ritual appeared to be more of a case of needing to demonstrate how intelligent they were in order to be accepted by their elders and not mocked due to their dress sense. Their ceremony continued with them strolling up and down the platform eyeing each other up, placing a mobile phone next to their ears but not speaking nor dialling. They would roll a tab and act camp, and basically give you an invisible two–fingered salute if you made eye contact with them; they were quite proud to know that you knew they looked scruffy. You see, they learn through strict fraternity style rulebooks not to ever look at themselves in a mirror. They must get dressed in the dark wearing clothes that come to hand without worry of style or being coordinated in any way shape or form. They do however have one dress code to adopt. Males must look gay, females must look like extras from Prisoner Cellblock H and overall they must have an air and grace about them that you despise and yet they just love the fact that you do.

The train pulled in a few minutes late and I had to wait behind a tearful girl with a stupid posh accent humping two trunks onto the carriage that I was waiting to board (humping as in carrying and dragging and not as in having sex). She ignored the fact that I like everyone else behind her wanted to get on the train, and took her time by pausing, wiping her tears, and kissing 'mummy' and 'daddy', 'grand–ma–ma', and big brother 'Tristen', the pet poodle 'Poochy', and the butler 'James', the next door neighbour who tipped his cap in acknowledgment of her superior society standing, her doctor, her dentist, and the family milkman, and – oh for fuck's sake get out of my way you upper–class inbred bitch!

My ticket was valid for coach 'C', seat number 72. However typical me, I'd boarded coach 'C' from the wrong end and took twenty minutes before I finally reached my seat which of course was at the other end. Trains these days have ticket stubs placed on the top of all reserved seats to prevent those without a reservation sitting in them (I suppose it's a way to tell them to fuck off and find a non–reserved seat). It's a clearly visible and simple method to implement (well, in theory yes, but in practice, no). We as the dominant race on this planet are to be frank inconsiderate and rather crude. Thereby we ignore any regulations that are forced unto us. We believe in the saying *'rules are there to be broken'* and so we partake in a ritual of the argument or politely asking someone, "Excuse me, is this your seat?" when in reality we know for a fact it's not their seat because it's your seat. The ticket stub sticking out of the headrest matches yours, yet even though we abruptly sit in the wrong seat we never abruptly point out to those sitting in the wrong seat that they are sitting in the wrong seat. We never say, "That's my seat". We adopt a conservative and polite method of asking a question that needs no answer because we already know the answer. On this occasion I was on board a train full of *Uni-Youth,* the rebellious future leaders of our nation, and ones who most definitely will ignore all rules laid down before them. Basically they sit where the fuck they like. What's more striking is the fact that although they know they are in the wrong seat they appear reluctant to make any effort to move until they've been physically shown evidence to prove that they're in the wrong seat. At this point they will start to move, but it's a slow task, for the *Uni-Youth* are society outcasts who have no fixed abode and travel around with their entire collection of personal items. They have effectively entrenched themselves in your seat turning it into home from home. It takes an eternity for them to gather up all of their belongings, re-pack all of their books which they've strategically placed out on the table in front of them so all and sundry can see what thespians they are – another classic sign of having an inferiority complex.

The train was starting to slow down as it reached its next stop – Darlington – and finally I'd managed to work my way down the aisle to the far end of the carriage and find seat number seventy-two and guess what, yep it was already occupied.

For my pleasure the occupant of my reserved seat wasn't part of the *Uni-Youth* but a new age Greenpeace activist couple and their baby. I pointed out politely that they were sitting in my reserved seat, but I'm politely told back that the seat has no ticket stub sticking out of the head rest. Well I couldn't give a shit, my ticket said seat number seventy two, hippy wifey was in my seat, the train was packed, and there was no way I was going to stand all the way to London. However I fell victim to the fact that wifey was sitting with a bairn on her knee (hubby by the way hadn't moved, nor blinked to even register my presence), and so I sat opposite them next to an old biddy – who remarkably looked like Mrs. Doubtfire. Hopefully at each station the train was scheduled to stop, no–one would board to point out I was sitting in their reserved seat.

Now I usually prefer aisle seats, but was on this occasion was stuck next to the window and a view without a view to stare out of for the duration of the journey, while Mr. & Mrs. Greenpeace sat entertaining their kid, or rather the wifey did (the fatha didn't move, ignoring everyone, including his kid), and of course I had to inhale the balm or whatever substance Mrs. Doubtfire had sprayed on her decaying body to hide the smell of wee. It all made for a journey into hell.

I settled down with a copy of the local Sunday newspaper, a can of Red Bull, my notepad, and hoped that the journey would be smooth and more importantly quick. I scoured the papers looking for any juicy SAFC related gossip, and once I'd read about the 2–0 win over Reading the previous day, my concentration was suddenly disturbed by an overbearing number of voices talking extra loud – deliberately. It belonged to a group of kids talking all posh like slagging off the North East, and in particularly, SAFC. I wasn't sure if they were aggrieved Reading fans or 'born–again' Mags – established 1992.

However as I started thinking of a way to ignore these kids who in my humble opinion lived off of daddy's inheritance, or to have a go at them, my mind and attention was startlingly diverted. Without warning I suddenly felt very uncomfortable, extremely embarrassed and fucking alarmed. Wifey had just lobbed out one of her boobs for the bairn to munch on. Talk about being vain! She didn't have a care in the world. It was, it would appear to her, to be the normal thing to do – lob out your tits on a packed train without 'retiring' to the loos to do it in privacy. At least daddy's boys had shut up. As for me, well I was sitting opposite this 'event' and didn't know where to look. Well I did. I couldn't help but be drawn to her breast. Fatha still hadn't moved. His head was now buried deep into a book.

Obviously their partnership consisted of him doing his thing while wifey looked after the kid. Mrs. Doubtfire was smiling and staring full on at the bairn chewing away on wifey's nipple as if blessing the occasion, giving her seal of approval for lobbing them out in front of complete strangers. How brash? I have to say part of me found all of this pathetic, whilst the rest of me found it quite disgusting to be honest. After all, we're talking about a yuppie here. We're talking about a woman with an obvious lesbo dress sense, ugly, never worn make-up in her life, bucked teeth (yep quite possible a stereotypical Geordie lass), had probably chained herself to the gates of Greenham Common in her anti-nuclear youth, votes for the Green party, prides herself on living as nature intended, rather than some buxom blonde stunner with tanned skin and a ring piercing her exposed nipple. Maybe I'm ignorant of the ways of the world outside of the protective boundaries of the City of Sunderland, but I cannot suss out how someone could just lob 'em out in full public view. Isn't there some law against this?

Well this was quite a site and an opportunity not to be missed, so I put down my paper, picked up my notepad and started to scribble down the events on the train – and I suppose this chapter – while it was still fresh in my mind, though it took quite a while to complete. I guess you can sympathise with me on this on considering I was sitting next to a dead body smelling of wee and looking like Robin Williams in a wig, a fatha who was obsessed with his Mills And Boons novel rather than the fact that his other half is undressing in front of a packed carriage in order to let junior extract the milk from her sagging breast who had by now obviously dropped one – the bairn not the wifey. Now on this occasion the one who smelt it (me) hadn't dealt it (me again)! The boob was finally put away and heavens forbid Mr. Yuppie actually moved. He raised his head; he put down his book and actually paid attention to his child. Fucking hell, careful now I didn't want him to overdo it. In his wisdom, he thought it was best to try to rock the kid to sleep, probably so that he could get back to his love story more than anything else. But like, hello, the child had pooped. There was no way it was going to go to sleep unless its nappy was changed. But this was Mr. Yuppie, a member of the human race who obviously knew how not to bring up a child, and as such kept on trying to rock the kid to sleep. By now, though, the bairn was screaming. It was being forced into a sleeping position it didn't want to go into. It had shit its nappy and it needed changing. Maybe if they could've dragged their new age arses out of their seats – and my reserved seat – and changed the bairn's nappy, maybe it would have gone go to sleep, and more importantly at that moment, stop fucking crying. Could they not tell it had shat itself? Could they not smell it? I could. It fucking stank and mixed with the odour emitting from Mrs. Doubtfire, I was either going to vomit, pass out, or trip. I had to move as panic set in. If wifey could lob out her tits for all to see, I'm sure they could just as easily change the bairn's shitty nappy on the table in front of everyone too. As fatha continued to try and get the bairn to sleep, wifey turned to him and had the naivety to ask, "Do you think I should change him?" What! Are you fucking jesting woman. Of course you should change him. I suddenly stood up. It took Mrs. Doubtfire by surprise. I wasn't sure why I had jumped up so suddenly. Maybe I was about to throw up, or scream at these two new age laid back arseholes to get a grip on reality and smell the obvious, or grab the bairn and change its dirt ridden nappy myself. Mrs. Doubtfire got up to let me out and I headed off to the toilets followed by a very slowly drawn out stroll to the buffet cart for a flattened cheese and tomato sandwich for sixty-eight quid. The train was about an hour further into its journey when I'd left the 'war zone' and was approaching Peterborough when I finally built up the courage to return. Remnants of the odour was still fresh in the air, but by now either the kid had given up and fallen asleep due to sheer exhaustion or wifey had showed some common sense and changed it. Fatha was now back into reading his romance novel. Wifey was lying with her eyes closed, and the bairn was actually asleep. I closed my eyes and tried to settle down just as it started up again. Oh for fucks sake! No end of juggling with it, playing with it, talking to it, and cuddling it would stop it from shutting up. I knew what it needed. It needed a dummy in its mouth. This, however, was the yuppie couple from hell, this was a family trying to raise a kid the natural way, one that had some balls, and incredible patience not to give in and stick a soother in the kid's mouth. I can remember when my second daughter was born and how we decided we'd try not to give her a dummy, something that lasted all of two hours. At present I couldn't last another two minutes without doing something drastic.

The train was now pulling into Peterborough so I got up and pretended I was leaving the train and for the remainder of the journey south stood next to the toilets a few carriages away (it wasn't comfortable but it was quiet and the smell was remarkably fresh) and I wondered what the fuck I was doing. Was this worth the stress I was inflicting on myself? Was I embarking on some sort of shameless yet boastful, pretentious, and snobbish publicity 'stunt' for my book? Was I not just setting sail on a jolly and doing the one thing I hated more than anything else?

> "Hey look at me I'm on the box, I've wrote a book, I'm git clever me, you are like git jealous, but you'll buy me book 'cos its about Sunlun' you see and seeing that like all of us Sunlun' fans are like git brainless sheep who will follow our club anywhere and buy any old shit no matter how tacky it is, you'll be making me git minted yer knar."

Once the train had reached its destination – Kings Cross - I had to tube it up to Victoria to find my hotel, which was about one hundred yards from the main exit and yet took me over an hour to find it. I normally pride myself on having a sense of direction, always having a sixth sense when it comes to knowing which way to go especially in a strange environment. I blamed my lack of direction on the fumes I'd inhaled from pissy pants (Mrs. Doubtfire) and shitty pants (the new age kid). It was close to half past seven by now and slowly getting dark.

I checked into my hotel and rested for a while before beginning yet another journey, this time to find Tower Bridge and go see for myself the human spectacle known as David Blaine and the self inflicted starvation publicity stunt he was undertaking whilst being suspended in mid–air for around forty days in a transparent box!

X

"If a man says something in the forest and no woman is there to hear him, is he still wrong?"

I have to admit to being a fan of David Blaine and his *'magic'*. Whether or not it's *'real'* (ahem), he is one cool dude when it comes to demonstrating sleight of hand, or more recently bizarre Houdini style *'publicity'* stunts. This latest one certainly had captured the public's imagination so when in Rome as they say; I had to take a look.

Having settled into my hotel room and after showering, and grabbing a bite to eat, a few tube stops later, I was walking across Tower Bridge towards the masses surrounding Blaine in his glass coffin – which by being suspended in mid–air was a way of proving it was him, and that there was no way he could escape to grab some grub, especially from the sadistic sausage sandwich van parked below him (imagine the odour he must have been smelling and how tortuous that must have been).

As I descended some steps at the far end of the bridge I entered into what can only be described as *'Blaine's World'*, stepping into an environment that must have mirrored that of an early twentieth century travelling carnival and the shadier and somewhat satanic freak shows that were all the rage during the Victorian era. All walks of life had gathered to shout at this man in his glass box, to stare in awe at this freak of nature, to be conned into buying shoddy merchandise, get mugged, fight, argue with the police, buy some hot dripping fat in a stale bun, and anything else that tickled their fancy. I was amongst all of it and I was loving it.

An area directly below Blaine's tomb had been fenced off but you could enter it provided you didn't mind being frisked by the faceless security guards overseeing the *'adoring'* public – well his temporary home had been subjected to food being tossed at it, paint balls being splattered on it, golf balls being projected off it and someone trying to climb up to see him and allegedly cut off his water supply. Outside the cordon, people were amassed shoulder to shoulder – a pick–pocket's heaven; inside the prison there was sufficient room to at least swing a cat. As I walked towards his box looking underneath it to see if there could be some hidden area (and as the bottom wasn't transparent – up close it looked a bit suspicious and in my humble opinion deep enough to contain food and other sustainable items that could be accessed by a hidden trap door, which I'm sure a man of Blaine's calibre could open without anyone noticing), I almost lost my balance and fell over a tramp who I think was asleep – well if he was dead no one gave a fuck. A cat flew overhead meowing. Someone was swinging! A gang of what I can only describe as being stereotypical Ali–G *'Staines Massive'* had gathered below to show their support for a man they most certainly *'wespected'*.

"Booyakasha Daveed," one of them shouted.

Blaine looked down, smiled, and waved.

Someone else then shouted, "We facking larv ya. Wist 'am!"

Blaine made eye contact and waved.

Then from infront of me, "Day–vid, Day–vid owva ere might – far–king Chowsee larves ya." Translated – "David, I say David my good man, the Chelsea Football Club acknowledges you".

Blaine grinned, and gave a thumbs–up gesture.

The Chelsea fan looked back at the West Ham fan as if he'd got one over on him. David Blaine had waved at the West Ham supporter you see, but had given a thumbs–up to the Chelsea fan. I couldn't miss the opportunity and so surprisingly and spontaneously burst out "David – Fuck The Mags!" He looked directly at me, nodded and gave two thumbs–up just as someone grabbed my arm violently. No obscenities allowed. One of the security guards *'politely'* asked me to leave and seeing as he was the person the phrase *'built like a shit brick-house'* was coined from, I sheepishly did, but hey – David Blaine gave me two thumbs up, and nodded at my FTM – *'Fuck The Mags'* war cry. Blaine must therefore hate the black and white scum as much as me; henceforth he has to be an adopted Mackem.

I left the chaos satisfied that I had seen one of my err *'idols'* and headed up towards Piccadilly before calling it a night. The gig the next day was to be held in some sports bar near Leicester Square and seeing as I didn't know where it was, and that I had to be there by nine in the morning, I thought best to find it now while I was out to save time the next day, and therefore not turn up late. That was a wise move as it took me almost two hours to find the fucking place and when I did it was full of Yanks wearing their *'gridiron'* colours watching some game of *'football'* being played.

I returned back to the hotel and before attempting to go to sleep, made a few notes about the night's events, oh and I phoned the missus to tell her I was fine.

Upon checking out of the hotel the next morning, I bumped into my equivalent – err my nemesis, the invited Mag fan, a pie eating baldy Geordie checking out in his colours. I wasn't wearing mine (to be honest, I didn't fancy travelling on the tube by myself wearing red and white stripes and therefore being open to potentially all sorts of unimaginable torture and horrors from the hoards of Cockney wide-boys travelling up and down the tube looking for victims), but I decided to introduce myself and for the remainder of the day the two of us politely chin wagged with each other. He may have been a Mag but it was company and besides he had little animosity towards all Mackems so I buried my true feelings towards the barcodes. Besides, when we travelled back up to the North–East he was engrossed in Brian Clough's biography so he couldn't have been all that bad – a Mag that can a) read and b) reading about a Sunderland legend!

And so, arriving spot on nine o'clock a fat Mackem and a fat Mag enter the Sports Café in London's Piccadilly Circus and are welcomed like movie stars (well, we sign in and get a free cup of coffee). I put on my colours and hang around until someone tells us what to do. Slowly more and more people arrive, their colours giving away their affiliation. I end up talking to a smug Charlton fan who was ever so keen to talk about *'that'* game (you know the play–off final at Wembley 1998). Eventually however, someone calls us together and seats us around tables of five or six. The front two tables appear to have the so–called media darlings assembled – Manchester United, Newcastle, Liverpool, Tottenham, and Chelsea etc. I was put on the very back table with Birmingham, Ipswich, AFC Wimbledon, and Crystal Palace. The Blues fan made me feel quite insignificant really. I know lately I've had more downs than ups when it comes to supporting The Lads and that my priorities have changed, so much so that compared to this Brummy I was ashamed to be the representative Mackem. Brummy you see lived in Scotland but was a season ticket holder at St. Andrews and made what was a six hundred mile pilgrimage to each and every home game. Now that was loyalty and from my point of view nothing but sheer admiration from which I bowed down before him! However he returned the compliment (I think) by saying that I looked like David Dunn, which means nothing to me but as *'Dunny'* was dating some sexy looking model at the time, I took it as a friendly gesture. Did that mean I was now a babe magnet? Don't tell my wife! The Tractor Boy or rather Tractor Girl was a nice enough bird though judging by her eyes I wasn't sure if she was talking to you or me when she spoke. The Eagle was an angry young man (more of that later), and the Don wasn't a Don, well he was a Don but a rebellious one, a ginger haired, lisping anarchist, and an active member in the foundation of AFC Wimbledon. For the whole day he would look towards the *'real'* Don fan sitting on another table with nothing but contempt. Missing from this assembly of the odd to the ridiculous was a Man City fan, a Smoggy, a Pompey fan and a Wolf. Why? I don't know, didn't ask, and didn't care.

Basically the day's events revolved around being shown ten clips of famous premiership games, goals, players, from which we all had to choose our top three. This would then form the basis of Sky's documentary. After each round of voting was completed, we were all free to roam, head to the bar and wait until the next set of clips was shown or until you were called to do a one on one interview.

In all, I was interviewed three times, and each time for between two or three minutes. At every opportunity, I did my best to diss the Mags and promote my book. When the television show aired, apart from glimpses of my arm and the back of my head (thank God you couldn't see the bald patch); my only claim to fame lasted all of four seconds!

As Sky showed Eric Cantona scoring a *'solo'* goal for Manchester United against Sunderland in a 5-0 win at Old Trafford circa 1996, the bit the editors chose to use of me was, "We lost that day like we always do at Old Trafford."

And that was it! My journey down, the suffering of the new age family and a pissy old woman, my journey back in time to see Houdini escape from a glass box, my sharing a joke or two with football fans you'd normally want to twat, my efforts to promote my book boiled down to four seconds of me looking like a right arse. "We lost that day like we always do at Old Trafford." I just hoped those words wouldn't come back to haunt me. Anything I said to praise SAFC, slate NUFC, and promote *Why Do I Do It?* was left on the cutting room floor. The invited Manchester United fan was a guy called Mark Chapman who presented Radio 5's 606 phone-in on weekends, a person who I swore had interviewed me on radio before regarding a forthcoming game between Man. United and SAFC, though he couldn't recall it, but he was the only person I managed to offload a review copy of my book too. I left him my phone number and email address and asked that he let me know if he could publicise the book in any way shape or form. Well Mark I'm still waiting for you to get back to me, many thanks - not. Allegedly, certain fans were supposed to be celebrity calibre. Apart from Man. United (radio presenter), the only other celebs present was the Liverpool fan - *'Romeo'* from the inner city hip hop group *'So Solid Crew'* whom I went nowhere near due to the size of his bouncer, and *'Shovel'* the Arsenal supporter.

As I sat down for some lunch with Baldy Geordie - a free buffet provided by the television folks - Shovel asked if he could join us, mainly out of curiosity wanting to know how two venomous and opposing supporters could eat at the same table let alone the same building. Shovel is/was the drummer from nineties pop band *'M–People'*; a group that he said never spilt, they simply took a break. He's had one hell of a holiday. He is also a guest on Sky's Soccer AM show almost every other week, something I asked him about e.g. do you have shares in the programme or fancy Tim or Helen (Lovejoy and Chamberlain)? His view on that was down to the fact that Soccer AM finds it hard to get *'celebs'* on the show who actually know what they are talking about. Shovel knows his stuff when it comes to Arsenal, but jested that certain guests are given a crib sheet to memorise as they get taxied into the studio – a set of notes reminding them of who they support, their latest result was... their star midfielder is called... and that way they don't look like prats when the cameras roll.

After lunch the same format continued, though for the duration of the proceedings the cameras remained pointing at the Liverpool, Man. United, Chelsea, Newcastle, and Arsenal table.

Out table was one man short. Angry Eagle had fucked off in a fit of rage. When it was his turn to be interviewed one on one, Sky were interested in a certain match played at Selhurst Park starring Eric – *'Jackie Chan'* – Cantona – remember that one? Angry Eagle wanted to talk about Palace but Sky wanted to talk about King Eric.

Angry Eagle therefore lost his rag. He was adamant you see that a game played at a later date which I can only assume was between Palace and United resulted in a Palace fan being stabbed to death and this incident he swore occurred as a direct result of Eric Cantona's theatrics (I've no idea if this is true or not as I've scoured the web looking for a story relating to this and could not find anything to substantiate his claims).

He was however so wound up that he lost all sense of control and started to threaten the director and basically anyone else who thought they were hard enough.

He was escorted off the premises or stormed off in a huff, never to be seen again.

Wow.

Football fans certainly are passionate folks – aren't we?

Anyway that was it, my little trip down South, a gig I managed to get Sky to cover costs for – which other fans hadn't *'demanded'*. I had lunch with a bloke who occasionally appears on telly, and a member of a successful pop band in the nineties, offloaded one review copy of my book which turned out to be a complete waste of time, but had managed to get David Blaine to acknowledge and I suppose bless our FTM war cry. Oh and I also managed to get my fat face on telly for all of four seconds. Was it worth it? Probably not, but it was an interesting *'adventure'* and introduced a roaming Mag to cyber squat on the SMB even though he had an illegal email address. Sites that offer free email addresses allow you to be totally anonymous on the World Wide Web are forbidden when it comes to registering to use Ready To Go's message board. That includes the likes of Yahoo and Hotmail. However it's not what you know, but who you know, so even though Baldy Geordie only had a Yahoo email address I managed to allow him to register through the back door – what, me doing a favour for a Mag? Am I finally mellowing? Those chill pills must have been tripping me no end when I did that.

My Dad Went To London

By J. O. D. Han

On Sunday my dad went to the train staitsoin. When he came home he told my mam that he is going to go to London because he is going on the TV because he roat a book called Why do I do it eny way when my dad got to the train staitsoin he got on his train and set off! to London. When he got there he went to his hotel he thought it was very nice. He had his own bathroom, TV, cetle, biscuk and a playstaitsoin and a bed. When it was dark my dad went outside and not far from his hotel was david blane in his box, so the next day my dad went to his train and came back home he told me all about it he thought it was great. The end.

My youngest daughter J. O. D. Han wrote this *'story'* in the car on the way home (once I'd been picked up from Durham station), and it's just so sweet I simply had to include it, warts and all!

XI

"The older I get, the better I used to be!"

All is quiet on New Year's Day, though a fluffy Anton wanted to get up at 6.00am and play. Thankfully I had no hangover. I'd gone to bed before midnight (sad bastard eh?), and for once, seeing as it was January 1st there was no footy. An exciting F. A. Cup tie against *'The Monkey Hangers'* (Hartlepool United) was just around the corner, a game without Marco Gabbiadini playing, (although he did make a half time appearance to the chants of *"Ole"* – and shortly afterwards announced his retirement due to injury). I decided that this year would be the one where I'd pull myself together, remove my bitterness, and become more optimistic about everything. I actually pondered over whether or not to Fung Shue the house or something, either that or light some black candles and perform some sort of satanic ritual to summon numerous hideous creatures to ward off my own demons (better than praying as far as I'm concerned).

Anyway fast–forward to the cup–tie and for the first time this season the Stadium of Light looked full. Over 10,000 Monkey Hangers were present – where the fuck did they come from? Hartlepool's average gate is only around 6,000. Thankfully all the so–called *'Hoolie'* talk on the web and press paranoia about trouble failed to materialise (apparently if you believe the rumours, a *'Warriors'* style meet was going to take place somewhere between a number of local firms – 'Pool, Darlo', The Gremlins, The Casuals). I did however notice a bloke get twatted on the way out, his nose bursting in a shower of blood spraying from his face and down onto his clothes (no colours). He stumbled over to the police (a large presence) who basically didn't give a shit about his unfortunate predicament.

As for the game, well it wasn't exactly one–sided. Sunderland without Arca and Poom would probably have been beaten as Hartlepool had the better of the play (in my opinion). Then again it could be said that the finishing was the issue. Sunderland could easily have been 3–0 up by half time, but as usual Stewart hit the woodwork – a talent he mastered during the 2003/2004 season at home along with John Oster. The weather was cold, but dry, and I wasn't too chilled by the temperature as I'd bought a Black Cats ticket with padded seat and access to the Black Cats bar – which to be honest you don't really need a pass for as it's piss easy to sneak in there on match days – with all the redundancies there just isn't enough staff to man the doors, and annoyingly there isn't enough staff to serve alcohol – only one bar open and a full house!

I went to the game with an old work mate, ending up sitting in row one of the designated Black Cats section of the ground, which I have to say was a great view. Unfortunately I had to endure the pleasure of sitting next to a Charva – a term which to be honest confuses me. I don't like saying Charva as to me it's a Geordie phrase and one that sums up a large proportion of the unemployed youth living in Tyneside. Charvas are primarily the out of work, don't give shit, attitude problem youngsters of Newcastle, though for some unknown reason their style and culture has spread across the nation like a disease, the term being modified and altered depending upon the city of residence – Spides, Scallies, Barries, Jacks, Meaders, NED's (non educated delinquents).

So what exactly is a Charva? The Tyneside version is described as follows, something I found on some dodgy looking web site (though you may have come across such characters where you live, including unfortunately the City of Sunderland).

Charva: Homo Charvaneus

A Charva is scum, filth, the level of humanity that you stand on in the grass. They are worse than shit. They are sometimes blamed as the source of all known sexually transmitted diseases due to their obsession with unprotected sex. If you've never encountered one before, think back to your youth, for the Charva was commonly the 'popular' *one at school whom everyone wanted to be and was really jealous of. They were being raised by Charvas and as they turned sixteen they would become fully-fledged Charvas themselves; and in most cases, with their own Charva offspring! Hopefully by the time you left school you will have realised that they were a waste of space and that you were better than they could ever have been. You may have gone on to get a good job, gone to college or university and gained a degree or something else of academic note. The Charva, however will not have, they only know how to do certain things and will turn out to be hairdressers or beauticians or in the case of the male population, dole mongers. Charvas dwell on rough council estates, primarily eat fast food, a diet high in fat and of no nutritional value.*

So how does one spot a Charva?

Well they can usually be seen hanging around on Friday nights drunk on half a bottle of cider, asking you for money of shouting "Who ya lookin at, d'ya wanna fight?" or, "Mista can ya gan an gerris some booze an some fags?" as you try to muscle past them into your local Spar to get some tea bags. These places are commonly known as hook-up spots (along with Grey's Monument and many parts of Monkseaton or Cullercoats – allegedly).

Compose yourself before replying, "fuck off you piece of shit and go and get it your fucking self."

However this method of retort will unsurprisingly fail. You see, they won't back away as they are probably used to being confronted and will probably surround you. You will know this is happening, as you will be able to see the flash of gold gleaming off their brightly coloured tracksuits. This is a common occurrence in large Charva ganglands and as you will come to realise, they never fight alone. Charvas are too scared to take on anyone themselves; they have to get their group to help them out. This is mainly due to the fact that they are soft as shite and wouldn't dare do anything outside of their posse.

So what about the characteristics? What do you look for when trying to avoid a Charva?

Well for girls they always have huge fringes, which they curl using a baked bean can. There are always massive amounts of gold dangling from their necks usually with tacky things such as dolls or clowns on them. They wear unnecessary large earrings the size of the millennium wheel that would rip the lobe off any normal person, and at least two sovereign rings on each and every finger.

They always wear tracksuits, brightly coloured or all white. Some now have turned to denim and check shirts, with fake Burberry scarves and baseball caps. Girls wear heavy eye make up and orange foundation, and have their noses and eyebrows pierced. They smoke heavily and drink cider or Tenant's Super on street corners, usually within spitting distance of the local corner shop. Girls usually have a large family of bastard children by the time they turn twenty-one.

On Tyneside when the temperature hits the minus figures the female of the species will feel drawn to wear mini or micro skirts that barely cover their arses, while the male Charva will wear a short-sleeved t-shirt of the designer variety.

Boys usually with short cropped or shaved heads, have their eyebrow pierced, and attempt to grow facial goatees, and if of a legal age, will turn up in their over the top 'sports' cars, which is usually an old clapped out 1100cc Ford Fiesta made out to be an XR2 (the thin tyres being a dead give away - unless they've managed to half-inch a set from a real XR2), though one mustn't forget the growing trend of Charvas purchasing Vespas - a hairdryer on two wheels.

The four wheeled variety however will have large body graphics, blacked out windows – tattooed cars, playing Blazin' Squad (who are a 'celebrity' Charva gang) music from a 5,000 watt stereo system, which simply comes across as 'bum, bum, bum, bum' due to the volume being turned up beyond distortion levels. They'll park wherever they feel like, simply to hang out.

Actually there was a story about the Ferrari Formula One team looking to employ some Tyneside Charvas when they found out they were able to remove a set of wheels from a car in under six seconds and without the proper tools (the Ferrari team do it in eight seconds with the proper tools). This move was seen as giving Ferrari a massive advantage as most races on the F1 circuit are usually won or lost in the pits. Unfortunately during the crew's first practice session, the Charvas were not only able to change the tyres in under six seconds but within about twenty–five seconds had re-sprayed, re–badged, and sold Michael Schumacher's Ferrari to the Williams Team for a dozen bottles of Woodpecker, 20 Lambert & Butler King Size, and two tubs of Evostik. Ruebens Barrichello's car was left standing in the pits on bricks with no wheels.

Note also an obsession with Rockport shoes (rockies), white trainers (Reebok classics), Henry Lloyd or Fred Perry hooped jumpers, getting into twenty years debt by purchasing expensive goods from Crazy George's, buying the latest police camera action DVD from HMV, or discussing who is the better action star out of Jet Li or Vin Diesel.

Teenage Charvas, especially boys, must tuck their track suit bottoms into their socks, a weird fashion trend, surely a clear signal of Charva status.

Then we have their kids and their doubled barrelled names – a must for any Charva parent (normally Tracey and Kevin). Girls' names range from Britney–Christina, to Daniella–Candice, to Janine–Charmiane, and boys Lee–Brandon, Romeo–Tyson or Dean–Brooklyn.

I ended up sitting next to one such Charva at the Hartlepool match. He was wearing a white shell suit, sovereign rings and Burberry baseball cap. Seeing as he appeared to be on his own, he didn't show any attitude towards those sitting around him. However I ended up getting my face badly scratched from one of his rings as we jump up to celebrate Julio Arca's goal – and the only goal of the game, his fist punching skywards and thus clipping my face. "Soz mate" he declares. It was an accident so I just graciously nod in his direction, while thinking to myself, "You're not my fucking mate (I haven't got any)."

The fourth round of the F. A. Cup beckoned. Sunderland had now won four games in a row, an incredible unbeaten run over the Christmas period, which I believe is something of a rarity and as such we were primed to catch the top two and steal that all important automatic promotion spot. Following a fifth success win (1–0 over Nottingham Forest – Arca once more the saviour), second place was within touching distance, something I, like many other fans, would not have foreseen a few months earlier. However, we're talking about Sunderland AFC here and an average Sunderland AFC at that (in a division full of average teams). No one was taking the division by the scruff if its neck and running away with the title. If consistency could be found we could do that. The transfer window was back open and regardless of debt, maybe a bit of speculation was required to take us back into the Premiership at the first attempt. Next match, Millwall 2 Sunderland 1 (catch-up exercise on hold). Hopefully this minor glitch would be dealt with once the next round of the Cup was out of the way and from my point of view, an exit. The draw was unkind to Sunderland pitching us against Ipswich away – no glamour tie against Man. United – that's what I'd like to have seen just to re-unite Roy Keane with his former mentor Mick McCarthy, plus of course joker in the pack and Sunderland skipper Jason McAteer. Surprisingly we won 2–1 (Arca scoring again) and suddenly we were in the 5th round. I could feel a nosebleed coming on! The draw was made and a home tie against premiership opposition was rewarded to Sunderland – gasps of "yes", but it was Birmingham City – gasps of "fuck". However such opposition was beatable and would mean Sunderland had a great chance to make it into the quarter-finals and of course for the fans find their voices, throwing the usual abuse at the entertaining wind up merchant known as Robbie (or depending who you listen to, Lily) Savage. That game was a while off just yet; we had league business to turn back to and a must-win game at home against Preston North End. In my opinion all league games were now must win situations. If we were to become serious challengers, games like this and no disrespect intended, should be as I've previously stated, bread and butter matches – guaranteed three points. Alas the game was called off at the eleventh hour (much to the disappointment of many who had travelled up unaware of the torrential downpour that our state of the art stadium with under soil heating and so on just couldn't cope with. "Standing water" the official excuse).

The disappointment of the postponement would soon be forgotten as news broke the following day that Bob Stokoe had died. I think most people knew the bloke had been poorly for quite a while, but it was sad to hear of his departure from this corrupt planet of ours. The man as dubbed *The Messiah*, and of course was the man in charge of the team that won the F. A. Cup in '73, and a game many still see as being the biggest ever cup upset in the history of the competition. Web-wise the condolences came pouring in, even the Mags honoured his death and respected the man for what he had achieved. The official Sunderland web site opened up an online book of condolence, which I found slightly perplexing. Instead of just leaving a message and your name, the online guest book was more like an application form wanting your name, address, email, post code, date of birth, telephone number and then your comments. Was this a genuine book of condolences or an excuse to gather potential marketing information and spam people with offers to buy tickets, merchandise and Club related news and information? That was my thoughts, not that I know if they were true or not, if not then why not just have a form that asks for your name, where you're from, and your comments. The next home match was thus the Birmingham cup-tie, seeing as the Gillingham league match was postponed due to international call–ups. A two–minute silence in honour of Bob Stokoe was to be made prior to the game with flags flying at half–mast – due respect. Stokoe died aged 73, we won the cup in 1973, and therefore superstition was slowly declaring that this year we would win the Cup again!

XII

"Too many freaks and yet not enough circuses".

Many offline people who read *'Why Do I Do It?'* have asked about the SMB and the type of conversations (also known as threads) that take place on there. Much like my categorization of the types of people who use the Internet and in particular the varying breeds of online Mackems, one can easily rank together the majority of threads posted on the SMB into four distinct groupings, *'the typical RTG warped humour style thread'*, *'the total football thread'*, *'the politically motivated, heated debate thread'*, and *'the threatening thread'*. I've taken actual examples of threads that fall into these categories indicating user names and their status – e.g. a Mackem, a Mag, a passer by, a moderator or an administrator and reproduced them in this chapter in an attempt to convey the passionate environment the online community produces.

The Typical RTG Warped Humour Style Thread

Subject: Bitter Elitists Mag Scum

MACKEM DJ (Mackem): *On the subject of home reserve games being at New Ferrens Park, some elitist scum bag nobsack writes on an NUFC web site*

"With the Mackems at home up the road at the dark place, we were spared the unwanted intrusion of red necks, but were still 'entertained' by a small group of City ne'er do-wells, who may have taken the night off from a nearby fairground to be with us..."

You know it always makes me laugh to see Geordie Mags put their Durham compatriots to the sword. Ouch.

PAULLY (Mag): *But that NUFC web site is the best website in the whald – FACT!*

WBM (Mackem): *But this is the best message board in the Whald – FACT!!!*

KEITH S30S (Mackem): *I agree, but the tiny hamlet of Whald only has the one website!*

THE STREAKER (Mackem and SMB Moderator): *Best website in the whald – FACT! – well fuck off onto it then (I shall process your termination forthwith).*

THE EXILE (Mackem): *Holy shit, does being a mod mean you have access to Terminators? Modern technology, eh? Could you not arrange for Mr Shearer to meet Mr. Uzi Nine Millimetre?*

THE STREAKER (Mackem and SMB Moderator): *He did and he bored the bastard to death.*

BOO BOYS (Mag): *Nine Millimetres? Why bring the length of your cock into it?*

GK (Mackem): *Because it's bigger than yours!*

BOO BOYS (Mag): *Fair point!*

[Ironic humour, black humour, or just toilet humour? This is a classic example of how topics can be made somewhat funny and shows the witty retort the users of the SMB can have.]

The Politically Motivated, Heated Debate Thread

Subject: Is this really that controversial?

TOON TOON (Mag): *Jenny Tonge has been asked by Liberal Democrat leader Charles Kennedy to quit his front bench following her remarks about Palestinian suicide bombers. She was speaking to a pro–Palestinian lobby when she allegedly said of Palestinian suicide bombers:* "I think if I had to live in that situation – and I say that advisedly – I might just consider becoming one myself." *Is this really that controversial? – I don't think so*

EL MATADOR (Mackem): *So do you condone people who commit suicide by blowing themselves up while taking out as many others (usually innocent) as possible – Iraqis, Afghans, Indonesian, etc. or just Palestinians?*

TOON TOON (Mag): *I'm sorry but where did I or she say that? I didn't, she didn't. She said she could understand why people do it and put herself in the same situation she said she could see herself doing it. She doesn't say it's right, she doesn't condone it. Read the words not what you want to read.*

SPLODGE (Mackem): *The point she was making was that one side has tanks, bombs and sophisticated weaponry to fight with and the other has a peashooter. She wasn't saying it was right just that they have nowt to fight back with.*

THOMAS HAUSER MD (Mackem): *Exactly – all she was trying to do was highlight how desperate these people must be to take that option. It's just bloody idiot journalists trying to whip up controversy when there's none to be found once again.*

72

24/02/79 (Mackem): *A fair point she's made, but a bit insensitive from the point of view of the victims' friends or family.*

JONNY B (Mackem): *Fair play to her. She's my MP so I'm a bit biased anyway. If the killing technology had been available in the ghettoes and concentration camps between 1935 and 1945, I could fully understand the Jews blowing up themselves and their oppressors.*

EL MATADOR (Mackem): *I don't see any condemnation of it, but an empathy with Palestinians. I wonder if she has empathy with the Indonesians who blew up the nightclub on Bali or the almost daily suicide bombings in Iraq or the People who flew planes into American cities? They would argue the same, that they were fighting against sophisticated weaponry of opponents and had no other methods at their disposal. Empathy with suicide bombers is controversial. She should not be surprised when people find it so.*

TOON TOON (Mag): *She was talking at a pro-Palestinian meeting. Why the fuck would she mention Bali or anything else? She said in their situation she could see herself doing the same, why try and drag it out to other situations?*

JONNY B (Mackem): *Difference being that Al Quaeda are fighting for a warped fanatical theology; the Palestinians are fighting for a share of what is rightfully theirs just as Israel did before 1946. Israeli statesman Minarkin Begin blew up the King David hotel as an Israeli terrorist in the 40's remember. It's bizarre and wrong to tar them with the same brush as Al Quaeda in my opinion.*

EL MATADOR (Mackem): *Because the same argument could be used by others to justify suicidal murder. Would it be right? Or just in the Palestinian situation?*

TOON TOON (Mag): *You asking her or me? I don't know her opinion but all she said was in that situation she could see herself doing it. If she was in another situation then she might do the same she might do something differently. Why isn't she allowed to say something without people assuming she actually means something* *else or that she condones the actions of other people they haven't mentioned?*

EL MATADOR (Mackem): *You obviously don't agree with Al Quaeda but do with the Palestinians so therefore in one case it's understandable and in the other it's not! Same method can be right and wrong depending on the cause. "Share of what is rightfully theirs" is your opinion which you are entitled to, but don't be surprised if everyone doesn't agree with you.*

GAV MACKEM (Mackem): *This definition of this 'war on terrorism' we have at the moment is totally farcical. This war should be against Al Quaeda. For fuck's sake, where would George Washington, Menachem Begin and Gerry Adams have been otherwise? The Palestinians are fighting to get their own land back and the suicide bomber is their only weapon of choice apart from a few home made rockets we would hardly use in a firework show. When you give people no hope and stall on giving the land back over a twelve year period of negotiation, continue annexing their land by building settlements and on top of that an apartheid wall nicking another fifteen per cent of the West Bank encircling all their major population centres it's no wonder they have no hope and want to kill themselves to fight back. I agree with her totally, fair play for her to speak out, she's got my vote!*

EL MATADOR (Mackem): *All I am saying is that if she as a politician publicly shows empathy with suicide bombers she should not be surprised that some find it very controversial. Which is what you asked in your first post, you didn't, others do. The other question I'm asking is: would she be as empathetic with Iraqi, Sri Lankan, Indonesian, etc. suicide bombers? I might be wrong but I feel she may not be as 'understanding'. Whatever the 'cause' the question is, is it right or wrong? My opinion is that it is wrong.*

TOON TOON (Mag): *But has anyone said it isn't wrong? I think it's wrong but that doesn't mean that if I was in the identical situation I might not do it. Don't confuse the issue. The issue is she says she could see herself doing it in that situation. You have tried to drag it out to other situations and now are trying to suggest she is saying* *that somehow it's right, she hasn't said that. This is the point of my original post, read what she says. It's not controversial in my opinion. Once you start making up things about what she is actually saying then it becomes controversial.*

JONNY B (Mackem): *I agree with everybody's right not to live in dire poverty under the yoke of a bullying and oppressive regime, and that is a right that should be extended to Israelis and Palestinians. Nowhere in my post did I condone suicide bombing, I simply said that it's more understandable when you are threatened with extinction and have zero quality of life. While we are on the subject of Israel, It is a statement of fact that Arial Sharon is a war criminal. As general in charge of the invasion of Lebanon he ordered the massacre of hundreds of refugees in the Shadrach & Shatileer refugee camps. He should be alongside Milosovic in The Hague in my humble opinion. The mess in Israel and Palestine will never get sorted as long as he's there. I appreciate that some people don't agree with the Palestinians having a share of a country that they have shared with the Israelis for 10,000 years although to be quite frank it beggars fucking belief. We live in a time where Jack Straw can't even say the word Palestine without being castigated by the Capitol Hill lobby.*

WAYNE JENNINGS (Mackem): *The same could be said about the IRA and their conflict with the British army occupying Northern Ireland for the thirty odd years' oppression from the British forces, so the Catholics decided to form the 'provos' and protect themselves from the enemy. I'm catholic and if I saw my father beaten or mam assaulted by a soldier or policeman just for being catholic or standing up for my rights such as employment or decent housing, I'd want to do something about it – anyone would but probably draw the line at suicide bombings.*

SMALLY (Mackem): *Whether or not she was right to say it is immaterial. She said it and has now been sacked. This is yet another example how our country is being eroded and destroyed from within. Personally I applaud her for speaking her mind yet as it doesn't conform to what her boss thinks or more importantly what the voters may think she gets the boot. I always thought that we had freedom of speech in this country. I don't want to get drawn into an argument* *about the wrongs and rights of Israel's occupation of Palestine or that Israel think that Palestine belongs to them or whatever. She was speaking as a human being with feelings, which is more than a lot of her ex–colleagues have.*

SIDESHOW BOB (Mackem): *So it's all right to say you understand suicide bombers as long as you don't condone it. Fine, I understand the reasons for 911, the holocaust, the IRA, the genocides in Kosovo and Rwanda etc. Bollocks. There is absolutely no reason to blow innocent people up. It is not to be condoned, agreed with, empathised with, or which ever other way you want to word it. How can you* '**understand**' *suicide bombers or any kind of terrorist? I've grown up in a working class area with high unemployment and low wages. But it hasn't turned me into a communist.*

CORKMAN (Mackem): *Hmmmm, she did actually condemn suicide bombers. However, as everyone is afraid of being called an anti–Semite, there has been an overreaction. Free speech does apply in this area? By the way, Sharon and his buddies were responsible for killing dozens of British soldiers in the 40s. People have no problem dealing with them. Even amateur psychologists know that desperate people do desperate things – has she ever actually justified suicide bombings? No. If I were living in the West Bank, maybe I would do the same? What is really scary is that many of the recent suicide bombers come from the middle class – the people who we would expect to support peaceful change – teachers and lawyers. Maybe the NHS is full of rampant lefty anti–Semites but I didn't meet anyone at work today who thought what she said was really outrageous. Stupid yes. Crass yes. The whole situation on the West Bank, the Gaza strip has created a huge well of people ready to be twisted, turned to do these things. 'Will you die for the cause? If you were going to die, wouldn't you like to take your enemy with you' seems to be the logic?'*

RANDY OSTRICH (Mackem): *I take it religious zealotry and fanaticism doesn't include building an apartheid wall, or bulldozing homes, or shooting schoolchildren, or foreign aid workers, or illegally occupying land, forcibly creating thousands of refugees all because some invisible guy in the sky supposedly said the land was yours 2000* *years ago? And when you look at it like that, yes, I understand how decades of oppression could foster the resentment required to kill not only yourself but many innocents as well. Condone: no, understand: yes. She expressed a view that broke no law, no parliamentary rule, overstepped no boundary and yet has been sacked from her job. Speaking her mind has not only cost her job but also cost us yet another freethinking politician.*

[This topic rolled over into twelve web pages before being archived, but goes to show how current affairs can dominate even the simplest of football forums and spark a debate full of strong emotions.]

The Threatening Thread

Subject: Anyone getting abusive private messages?

LDL (Mackem): *Anyone else getting abusive private messages from RWI? Apparently if you write anything that criticises the bloke he responds in the traditional Neanderthal way of spouting abuse at my family and me. Just shows the quality of the bloke when he starts abusing my kids as well. He seems like a very sad bloke if you ask me. How sad can it get?*

From: RWI
To: LDL
Subject: Wanker

You cock sucking ugly wanker. I hope all of your family go blind and start bumping into each other. Tit.

RWI (Silly Adolescent): *Just you, ya sad ugly twat.*

THE BANDIT (Mackem): *He is just a complete wanker in all honesty. His net contribution to the board is 'Fuck off' and 'so'. He reminds me of Kevin out of Kevin and Perry to be honest.*

KING AL (Mag): *Well RWI I've never had a problem with you myself, but that's well out of order.*

LEONARD OSBOURNE (Mag): *Oh dear. RWI, you are obviously a wanker, and you must be ugly!*

RWI (Silly Adolescent): *So LDL gets on his high horse and goes on as if he's better than me – he does read The Telegraph you know. The bloke's a tit. He didn't have to make such a shit comment to my post that 'I read The Sun'. Both sides have got to be looked at. Besides, I'll only come back as a different user name.*

PENSHAW LAD (Mackem): *Sad, silly little boy.*

LDL (Mackem): *I never take threats against myself or my family light–heartedly mate. You meant it in my opinion. And now you try and crawl out of the embarrassing hole you have dug yourself into by saying it was light hearted. You sir, are a wanker of the highest order I'd say.*

RWI (Silly Adolescent): *I'm trying to crawl out of a hole? Like shite, I couldn't give a fuck man – it's a message board, get a grip.*

[Unfortunately such abuse continues all too often. Now although I've disguised some of the names of the people involved, this is your typical online cyber war where people verbally insult and abuse each other. The poster known as RWI was banned, came back in disguise as RWI2 (clever), was banned again and eventually completely blocked from using the SMB. The arrogance however was blatantly evident when RWI emailed RTG to ask why he'd been banned, demanding to be re–instated, instead of just apologising. His ban still remains.]

The Total Football Thread

Subject: Sheffield United Cup Ratings.

BRI (Mackem): *Well having watched a thrilling cup–tie that's put us into the Semi-finals of the FA Cup; here goes my ratings for the Lads in today's game.*

Poom 7 out of 10 – He was very good and did it when necessary.

Wright 9 out of 10 – Was outstanding, showing vast improvement this season and man of the match mostly in the second half.

Breen 7.5 out of 10 – Was committed but didn't win many clean headers.

Babb 7 out of 10 – Was as committed as Breen, but showed one or two little failings in the second half.

McCartney 8 out of 10 – Had an excellent game.

Oster 8 out of 10 – One of his better games, always gives the opposition something to think about.

McAteer 8 out of 10 – Excellent game.

Whitley 6 out of 10 – Hmm, not as good as he can be, a few poor passes today.

Arca 7 out of 10 – Fantastic in the first half, but pretty anonymous in the second.

Kyle 6 out of 10 – Sorry, didn't see him win a ball all game.

Smith 9 out of 10 – Super goal and excellent movement, could have had another in the first half.

The crowd 10 out of 10 – You make me proud.

REDCAR MACKEM (Mackem): *I thought Smith and Wright where outstanding today.*

EPPING (Mackem): *Sorry but McAteer was diabolical in the first thirty-five minutes. The foul he committed just outside the box was amateur, too many loose balls and very lazy looking passes – and I am a fan of his.*

BOOT CLEANER (Mackem): *Well I thought Kyle had a good game, chased the balls, won the balls, knocked them down and so on. But Babb, I'd give him 3 out of 10 – his foot resembles a sand wedge as he continually sliced the ball straight up in the air, but more annoying was that he constantly had his hands on the strikers, giving away possession.*

LANCHESTER RED AND WHITE (Mackem): *Babb had a really good game today. To argue otherwise is just gratuitously having a go at the lad. To go back to Bri's original rating, giving Oster 8 out of 10 is odd if you ask me as there was no end product from him and he was dodgy defensively in the second half.*

STRANGELY BROWN (Mackem): *Referring to Babb I thought Wayne Allison scared him, he panicked every time the ball was played up to the 'big chief' and had to resort to fouling him to get an advantage. We don't like 'big' centre forwards do we?*

TARTAN MACKEM (Mackem): *Exactly! That's what was pissing me off! I'm sorry but Babb was crap in my opinion. I thought Whitley and Oster were quite good, except Oster is a bit of a pansy when it comes to tackling (though Jeff more than makes up for that). Kyle was decent too.*

THE SAINTLY MACKEM (Mackem): *Can't we give them all ten out of ten? We're in the semi-finals of the F. A. Cup man!*

[This is a common thread where we all turn into professional soccer analysts and critics, though that's not meant as derogatory, more of a factual statement. Fans of any club will always formulate their performance of the team in their own

mind, and online post their views before entering into what is normally quite a sensible debate either full of praise or full of criticism.]

The Satirical Thread

Subject: Liked Despotic Dictators And Mass Murderers

TYNE VALLEY BLACK CAT (Mackem): *Let's be satirical, so who are your liked despotic dictators and mass murderers? I'll start. Anyone for Mussolini or Idi Amin?*

TR1P0D (Unknown): *Nah, George W. Bush!*

STUBBER (Mackem): *Mussolini made the trains run on time don't you know.*

TYNE VALLEY BLACK CAT (Mackem): *And with regarding to Benito he wasn't a Mag as far as I am aware, so he wasn't all bad.*

BRI (Mackem): *Ceaucescu the ex–dictator of Romania. Him and his wife nicked the gold taps from Buckingham Palace when he stayed there as guests of the Queen.*

ZAPATTATASH (Unknown): *Pol Pot had a season ticket at Sid James allegedly!*

STUBBER (Mackem): *You're not wrong there. The Khmer Rouge all stood in the Leazes End next to Tony Blair.*

BILL (Unknown): *Saddam Hussein: the un–cleaned must have liked him as a million of them marched in favour not to kick him out of Iraq.*

TYNE VALLEY BLACK CAT (Mackem): *Pol Pot had a season ticket at Sid James Park? That's a damned lie and you know it. He just borrowed a season ticket off his mate from Blaydon who didn't use it when they were live on Sky because he wanted to sample the superior atmosphere in his local.*

LOZMAN (Unknown): *Well it has got to be King Zog of Albania for me. A great name and of course he once banned men from wearing beards.*

IGOR (Mag): *Darth Vader wasn't that bad a dictator as well.*

SHEARER IS A W*** (Mackem):** *Well I quite like George Reynolds.*

FLARED HICKS (Mackem): *Vlad the Impaler, who was from Rochdale way or thereabouts gets my vote.*

---NEMO--- (Mackem): *Vlad was from Halifax mate and a season ticket holder as well. He was much maligned and misunderstood in my opinion.*

DAVE TOWERS WAS HERE (Mackem): *Ken Bates. In true BQF style he once said to assorted journalists,* "Right, I'm going home to my three hundred acre farm. You can bugger off back to your council flats." *Never a dull moment With Comrade Ken eh?*

ARCHIE BLAGGER (Mackem): *Vlad the Impaler would often act as matchmaker for the common man. When he saw a hard working chap, who was wearing shabby clothes he took pity on him. Vlad decided that this man's wife was not deserving of this hard working bloke, as this man's clothes were obviously not well maintained by his wife. So Vlad killed the old wife and then got an all-new harder working one for the gadgey. What a nice evil mass-murderer. Oh and he burnt all the useless noblemen of his country as well. The equivalent of getting Edward, Sophie, Fergie et al in a house and setting fire to it. Couldn't have been that bad a man.*

CORKMAN (Mackem): *SLORC! (State Law and Order Restoration Committee). The very brutal military types who run Burma/Mayanmar and obviously Bond/Mission Impossible fans if they give themselves a name like that. They are building loads of railway lines and holiday resorts – admittedly with slave labour, but no one is perfect.*

TRAVIS (Mackem): *Genghis Khan was good in 'Bill And Ted's Excellent Adventure' but I don't agree with his political morals, apart from the* "as much pussy as you can eat" *rule.*

[Satirical? Maybe. A thread that is amusing to some, bewildering to others, but evidence of just how varied a message board can be, especially when its sole purpose is to talk about football and in particular Sunderland Association Football Club.]

These examples show how colourful Internet *'chat-rooms'* can be whilst at the same time they show just how dangerous they can be. Whether it's a message board or a live chat room, the Internet is there to be enjoyed, something which these days is getting harder to achieve, and when venturing into the world of football, one must always be ready to handle oneself, throw caution to the wind, and be anything but green. Be weary for such environments in many cases are in reality electronic *'Fight Clubs'*.

XIII

"I see no joy, I see only sorrow, I see no chance of your bright new tomorrow!"

Having been persecuted by others and having persecuted myself for so long, 2004 was to be a good year. Well that's what I decided 2004 was going to be. Mind you, I wasn't wiping any slate clean or letting bygones be bygones, I just wanted to sort out my own shit, sort out the demons in my head, and try to look at life from a more positive point of view. A new year always provides the excuse to do something different or to start afresh, and on Sunday 4th January 2004, having seen The Lads defeat The Monkey Hangers the day before; I took the dog out for a walk and found a twenty pound note lying on the floor in the local cemetery. This is where I'd normally take Anton for his daily exercise. Seeing as there wasn't a soul to be seen it was a case of finders keepers, and maybe, just maybe a sign that 2004 was to be a good year after all.

I'd now been taking prescription drugs for over eighteen months and wanted desperately to wean myself off them. I was no longer depressed. I was angry. I had one bastard of a temper that I was trying to control, but I doubted anti–depressants would cure that. If anything they were the cause of it, an unwanted side affect of pumping manufactured chemical shit into my bloodstream on a daily basis.

A few weeks into January it was my eldest daughter's birthday and on the weekend prior (her birthday was on a Tuesday), we gave her a swimming pool party and I felt alleviated entertaining the kids splashing around, helping the little 'un to keep afloat, being the embarrassing dad that you're supposed to be when it comes to kids approaching their teens. I was the whale in the water; my uncontrollable and ever expanding beer gut a sight of embarrassment for me, and amusement for everyone else.

Another direct affect of taking anti–depressants in my opinion was my uncontrollable ability to put on weight. I had ballooned in size and yet I didn't eat that much. I drank a lot I'll admit that, but my weight had become such a concern that I used the New Year, as another excuse to diet and lose not only the beer belly but the man boobs I was growing.

On the Monday night before the bairn's eleventh birthday, having picked them up from school (that is after I'd finished work and collected the wife from where she works, yes unwittingly I am a taxi driver as well), I decided that we should all go to the local supermarket so she could choose a birthday cake for us to privately enjoy the next day. I thought it best to go home first so I could quickly take Anton out for a walk before setting off to the nearest ASDA.

And it is that moment and that decision that will haunt me for a long, long time. 2004 was to become anything but a happy new year. It was a very windy night and the cemetery looked and felt quite ominous as the wind rustled through the trees and whipped around the headstones that were still standing though decaying faster than those they represented six feet under. As usual I'd let him off his lead so that he could go mental, galloping around tiring himself silly and allowing him to do his business, which I'll point out I always picked up in little carrier bags to dispose of properly. I may not have done so in the past, but I was sick of seeing dog shit everywhere and thus thought if someone like me would make the effort them maybe those less angry and those less ignorant or less sociable would do the same.

After twenty minutes or so it was time to head back home, as I was sure he'd be quite hungry now and my daughter would be getting impatient. I turned to put his lead back on and head out of the cemetery, but he was nowhere to be seen. I had looked away for a split second and he was gone. He had disappeared into the darkness. I shouted in vain for him to come over, he was still young, but very intelligent, and never wandered too far.

Maybe the wind was throwing my voice or maybe it had spooked him. Either way panic was setting in as I backtracked desperately looking for him, shouting for him.

After what must have been ten or so minutes I ended up near to the cemetery exit and noticed two cars pulled up blocking the way in. I knew immediately what they were doing there. I didn't want to believe what my gut was telling me nor did I want to approach, but I had too, I had no choice but confront my worse fears. As I walked out, past the exit gates, there he was lying still on the pavement, a couple of people standing over him.

I bent down; the people around me asked if I knew whom he belonged too. And that's about all I remember. Even now as I write this, the rest is a blur. Somehow I got home, I wanted to take him but couldn't as the police had been notified and until they arrived, the scene of the accident couldn't be 'contaminated'. Somehow I told the wife and the bairns. Somehow I managed to go back to see him off as my father-in-law and brother-in-law drove him to some place in Gateshead that the vets had told my mother-in-law to take him (my wife quickly managed to phone them for help and support before she also became too distraught). Somehow I waited as the rain came down, waiting for almost one hour before the police came and before he could be driven off to his final resting place. Somehow I lifted him into the car, his neck limp, broken (hopefully it had been quick and instant and that he hadn't suffered). I just pray he wasn't panicking, looking for me as I panicked looking for him.

My wife, the kids, and myself, were all in fits of tears. Yes, I'm a grown man and yes I'm openly admitting here that I cried like a newborn baby that night and for a few days afterwards. The kids were hysterical. They had never experienced death before. This was our puppy, our cuddly loveable pet dog, a member of the Han family that we had purchased in order to have something good to focus on, something me and the wife could take out for romantic walks as the two of us tried to remain soul mates and ignore the harsh reality and bad luck cards that we'd been dealt in recent years.

Anton had been knocked down and killed as he tried to get home by himself – well that's what I perceived he had been doing, either way I blamed myself. I was the one taking him for a walk. I was therefore the one in charge of keeping him in toe. It was my decision to go home first before going to ASDA for a birthday cake. It was my fault that my daughter's birthday had now been completely ruined. The house was now silent, no barking, no chasing the cat, no clip-clopping of this paws, no shit or piss to wipe up, no Anton, and it was my fault.

The pain was beyond physical. The diet I was beginning to start was forgotten about as I ate and drank, or rather drank more than I ate to ease the pain. My wife never ate full stop, plummeting in weight, staying off work for a while and being prescribed anti-depressants herself.

Our life was once more in a mess, just when it seemed to be getting itself back on its feet, and it was all my fault. The kids stayed off school though for just one day. I plucked up the courage to take them to back as maybe the surroundings and the routine would help them cope and pull themselves together, something that kids are extremely resilient at doing and something from an emotional point of view us adults should be extremely jealous of. Besides there was little point in them sitting at home in silence, if my wife was going down the path I had followed I didn't want the kids to do so as well. Football, the Internet, my job, my writing, well that means nothing compared with a life, a life that had been cut short, a life that had been taken away from us.

Why?

Why us?

Why me?

Such mental trauma and such shit had continuously happened to me ever since 9/11. Someone somewhere had cast a curse on me that I couldn't shake. If there is such a thing as God, then why was he punishing me?

But then the reason and answer is obvious.

God doesn't exist.

If he did he wouldn't let such shit happen to me. He wouldn't allow earthquakes to erupt killing thousands, or murderers to commit heinous crimes, nor allow the outbreak of war, famine, and plague. If God existed, 9/11 would not have happened, the holocaust would not have happened; terrorists and suicide bombers would be figures of fantasy and not reality. The Middle East would be a peaceful place, my parents wouldn't have split, SAFC wouldn't have threatened me because of the actions of someone else, and Anton would still be alive.

I may not be religious – pretty obvious I guess, but I do sort of believe in fate and that although one can weave one's own destiny, fate is something we cannot control and as such there is a reason for everything, whether or not we can see any logic in the events that encompass us.

One week after Anton's death the phone rang and on the other end of the line were the people we'd bought him off. They wanted to pass on their sympathies with us, but also wanted to offer us a gift. Anton's parents had had another litter – by mistake – and they had one puppy, a boy with the same markings and the same colour as Anton.

He was ours to take if we wanted. What we were being offered wasn't to be a replacement for Anton. What we were being offered was in my opinion something to fill the gap left by Anton, and give us what we had had with Anton.

We were being given an opportunity to start over. Was this fate dealing a cruel hand or wiping the slate clean? Maybe 2004 could be a good year; maybe my 2004 followed the Chinese calendar; maybe I could start over and pull myself, no, ourselves together once and for all.

So we said yes, though initially we were very apprehensive about starting over.

Was it the right thing to do?

Would people think we were replacing Anton as if he had been some broken toy, a ready–made alternative?

Was this fate giving us another opportunity?

We had to wait a few weeks until he was old enough to come home. Anton was named after my admiration and fascination with the dark side, with satanic elements, or probably more to do with a fuck off attitude to all that is allegedly morally right and everything that I have been taught to respect that had been spat back in my face.

The new puppy was named Whiskey, a more traditional name for a dog, but I suppose I have to say that whiskey is the devil's brew and so maintains my affiliation with the dark side.

Whiskey may have taken over from Anton, but Anton won't be forgotten. Whiskey is not Anton; he looks similar but isn't as fluffy, has a different personality, and is not let off his lead. I don't think that is a cruel step to take, but I simply cannot take him out for a walk and let him loose.

I do take him in the cemetery, a baby step I took upon myself to do, to shake off the stigma of what it (the cemetery) had become, but I don't let Whiskey loose, I just can't.

I just hope when my daughters next birthday comes round we can enjoy the day rather than remember it for all the wrong reasons.

XIV

"One day I might just pull out a gun.
Plenty of candidates for the first shot!"

February meant fuck all to me in terms of football, what with
Anton being knocked over and killed. Take away the F. A. Cup
win against Birmingham at St. Andrews which was a fantastic
result, you're left with the game away to Watford that saw
Sunderland 2-0 down with 10 minutes to go before Darren
Byfield came on for his debut to score and level the game –
who? A lucky draw didn't mean luck would continue as the
team was demolished 4-0 away to Cardiff City (if you believe
the hype we lost the battle on the pitch but the Seaburn Casuals
flew the flag for SAFC off the pitch – err yeah right). It could be
argued that games like these, ones were we easily crumbled,
ultimately cost us promotion. A trend was emerging that in my
opinion was the cause of points being dropped – Cardiff City
away, Crystal Palace away, Norwich City away, Preston North
End home – the red card! The 2003–2004 season provided SAFC
with an epidemic of sending–offs. In some games, we held on
and won, others cost us valuable league points and of course a
place in the F. A. Cup final (more of that later). Not quite a dirty
dozen but an *'unlucky'* seven players found red more than once
and for some their suspensions arose from sheer stupidity. The
culprits:

Ben Clark (Huddersfield Town (H) League Cup) –
Deliberate Handball *(or rather save a goal from being
scored 'cos the defense was nowhere to be seen).*

Julio Arca (Sheffield United (A) League) – Second
Bookable Offence *(or shouting his fucking mouth off
prior to his brain kicking in).*

John Oster (Norwich City (A) League) – Serious Foul Play *(kicking the shit out of the opposition – who John Oster? – must've smuggled an air pistol on the pitch).*

Julio Arca (Wigan (H) League) – Second Bookable Offence *(or shouting his fucking mouth off prior to his brain kicking in).*

Kevin Kyle (Wimbledon (H) League) – Second Bookable Offence *(or shouting his fucking mouth off prior to his brain kicking in).*

Joachim Bjorklund (Cardiff City (A) League) – Professional Foul *(being a right dirty bastard).*

Jeff Whitley (Preston North End (H) League) – Violent Conduct *(or for killing an opposition player).*

Jeff Whitley (Reading (A) League) – Second Bookable Offence *(or shouting his fucking mouth off prior to his brain kicking in).*

Jason McAteer (Millwall (A) F. A. Cup) – Second Bookable Offence *(or for being a fucking stupid arsehole).*

Mart Poom (Crystal Palace (A) League) – Professional Foul *(or rather save a goal from being scored 'cos the defense was nowhere to be seen).*

The home game against Preston North End was winnable, but ended three all. With Whitely being sent off, and therefore being a man down, this red card it could be said cost Sunderland two points. The game away at Cardiff was over after twenty minutes once Bjorklund had been dismissed, and therefore a game with an unknown outcome should we have managed to keep all eleven players present and accounted for (let's say potentially a point dropped). And of course with Mart Poom being sent off at the game away to Crystal Palace, any chance of salvaging a point was instantaneously erased. The red cards weren't always one way traffic. The home game against Wigan saw Julio Arca dismissed at half time, the opposition taking the lead on seventy minutes before Sunderland salvaged a point through a penalty and the dismissal of one of Wigan's players, and another game where victory was there for the taking prior to kick off, and after ninety minutes we were left with one point for our efforts. All in all, we have an extra five points here, and five points that should've been added to our total tally and could have had if the players' self-restraint and discipline had been kept under control. Looking back at all of Sunderland's results over the course of the season, there are numerous other games that we could have and should have won, suspension to key players possibly costing us additional points, and seeing as we finished only six points behind runners-up West Bromwich Albion, the five points I've pulled out of the hat mixed with other obvious ones (e.g. we should have won the home games we ended up drawing in against the likes Stoke City, Gillingham, Crewe Alexandra, Coventry City, and Cardiff City to name just a few), then promotion – if not the title – was there for the taking. But this is Sunderland AFC, the club we love and worship, who never, ever do things the easy way. Well we have once, the record breaking 105 points Division One title winning season of 1998 – a fluke?

XV

"It's like watching a scene from One Flew Over The Cuckoos Nest!"

I found out the day before my birthday (the Monday morning following the one all home draw against Birmingham City in the F. A. Cup) that I was a tosser, a wanker, a disgrace, and should fuck off up the road and support the Mags. Many probably will say, "Oh yeah, that P D Han is a right tosser", but that's probably for other reasons. The fact that I decided not to go to the Birmingham game in the F. A. Cup, one match, made me, like many others suddenly a hated figure. I was no longer a fan, nor a supporter. In fact I, along with everyone else who did not attend that match should, according to the extreme die-hards be publicly stoned. This was more than just a game you see, it was a remembrance match honouring the recent death of Bob Stokoe, and therefore all fans had a duty to attend, failure meant your loyalty factor hit zero, regardless of how many games you had attended in your life, or how much money you had spent supporting SAFC, or how many miles you had travelled, or how many times you had bunked off school or called in a sicky in order to get to a match – not so much important ones but minor pre–season friendlies (I recall going to watch a 0–0 draw at Doncaster mid–Eighties where less than fifty SAFC fans turned up having phoned work to say I was unwell). That's an example though not an excuse. I see no reason to justify why I should have gone to the Birmingham game or why I did not. I guess finances (middle of the month), Valentine's Day (you know football fans are allowed – I think – to love more than one person, one person being the human form representing a football club), and being lazy, it was after all on the telly. Personally I was still pissed off with recent false hopes, I was still pissed off that the Club *'threatened'* to sue me because of the antics of some *hallway,* and that my loyalty counted for nothing because I was a scum of the earth fanzine editor, and that meant I had joined the ranks of the gutter press looking for any bit of gossip to spread and undermine the powers that be inside the ivory towers. My head was also full of tortuous nightmarish visions of running after Anton in the cemetery a few weeks earlier to no avail. February, remember, was for me a month where football, no matter how important a game or ceremony was to take place, meant fuck all. On the day of the Birmingham match, we had just brought home our new puppy, our Anton clone. I was still finishing off decorating the bathroom, I was still upset and still blaming myself for Anton's death, and I was still taking anti-depressants. However no matter what I say or write, all of the above falls into the category of excuses to the radical unreasonables, and petty ones at that. And because of this, I, and I suppose that's a collective 'I' for it encompasses all non-attendees that day (I'm just relaying the reasons why not from my own perspective), were suddenly no longer worthy of being SAFC supporters, I had to renounce any loyalty I had, all interests had to be forthwith stopped, my tattoos had to be removed by painful and expensive laser surgery, and by doing so, I would have purged my body of sin. Bollocks!

> *Be ashamed, very ashamed. Yes, it's a crapper that we've pulled the 5.35 kick off. Fair enough, that makes it nigh on impossible for some to travel and some might have to give it a miss due to prior evening engagements. But those who could be there but choose to watch it for nothing and get out on the lash sooner have no excuse in my book. Yes, many gave up their season tickets after years of inept management and false hopes. I can see their point and sort of understand their stance of not going to games to try to overthrow the Regime. But this game has nothing to do with that. It's about pride and respect. If you do choose to stay away, don't come back. You're not needed and not wanted. Go join the other designer 'fans' – The Mags and Man. United.*

To have your loyalty questioned on the outcome of attending one particular game appears to be a naive, rash, and rather pathetic attempt by some who appear to take pleasure in the low attendances the Club was suffering. They are moaners out there who don't want your excuses no matter how justified they are, you weren't there, they were there, so fuck off! Or were they there? I read a ridiculous amount of topics posted on the SMB from so-called fans questioning so-called fans for not going to this game. More interesting was the time stamp recorded on their posts, indicating they were either at the game typing up their vitriolic outcry on a laptop or PDA, or were in fact not there themselves thus using the exclusive anonymity the Internet offers to blame their non attendance onto others. Its amazing what you can say, do, and get away with on the Internet, you can after all be the world's longest serving, most loyal supporter the world has ever seen, you have been there, done that, got the t-shirt (in fact a closet full), in reality – outside of the Matrix – you may be nothing more than a spoilt fifteen year old sitting in his bedroom having never been to a match full stop, not aware that Roker Park actually existed – much like the Mags who knew nothing about the 'Toon' prior to Keegan arriving.

But that's how it works online, it's easy to wind people up, take a moral stance no matter how one-sided, and basically show any passing supporter or media reporter that Sunderland fans are a bunch of bitter people, resentful of each other, arguing for Christ's sake over ticket allocations, and who should or should not get a ticket for the F. A. Cup Final at Cardiff in May. Like, hello didn't we need to win the replay against the Brummies first? There's nowt wrong with dreaming of a glorious final, but to start playing the record again – if you didn't go to this game or that game then come May you don't deserve a ticket for the final, but I do so nah, nah, nah, nah, nah!

So everything boils down to this one game? Is it just me or do some people genuinely believe that others who didn't attend today need to justify themselves? Anyone can give reasons for not attending but the bottom line is you either choose to go or you don't. The one way we won't get the fans back is by insulting them. The Club require some sort of strategy to tempt them back.

It seems to me like SAFC are just shrugging their shoulders and accepting shite crowds instead of actually doing something positive about it.

We are calling the wrong people. We should be lambasting the Club for placing us, once more, in a situation where the fans feel totally and utterly let down. To all the stay-away fans I would say your message is coming through loud and clear. Unfortunately you probably aren't being listened to. SAFC is, in my humble opinion, run like a corner shop and I can see no obvious sign that the mentality is changing.

Rather than Murray reiterating over and over his enhanced commitment to stay, he should be reiterating over and over how he has failed the fans of SAFC and his absolute desire to depart the scene totally.

I sometimes wonder what proportion of the missing twenty thousand are your crushed and dejected followers who, after decades of betrayal by the club, have finally given up and – with a tear in their eye – turned away, in the hope that their sacrifice will somehow bring success to the team.

There is only one person to blame – our beloved chairman. When we were doing well he failed to invest and only did so in a last desperate gamble that failed magnificently. When we were up challenging we attracted casual supporters who wanted to be entertained and associated with success.

As any surfer knows you cannot ride a wave that has passed. Murray missed the wave and the new supporters are no more. Due to our finances it is difficult to imagine we will ever get them back.

For every sensibly constructed and well-argued point however, the World Wide Web answers such debate in a cynical, poor, and in fact pathetic fuck off reply;

Yeah but what proportion are simply not prepared to follow Sunderland when we're not doing well. Unless you had a genuine excuse you are a tosspot

The top and bottom of it is if we were playing Arsenal or Chelsea we would have had a full house. To the missing 20,000, fuck off and support the Mags.

No excuses for not turning up. I think the line has been drawn. Anyone there yesterday is a true fan; anyone not there (unless they have a genuine excuse) is a disgrace.

There are of course as you can see, two sides to every story, and football, well football generates passion unlike any other form of entertainment or pastime, thus you always get extreme differing of opinions. No one will see eye to eye.

So why are people who choose not to go to a single game a disgrace?

Well is hardly one game is it? We've been around the 25,000 mark all season. You've either been to all/most games this season or you haven't. Its as simple as that and to reiterate what most people are saying if you live locally and just aren't bothering to go or are making some sort of ridiculous statement to the board then you are the reason that we are open to ridicule from the Mags etc and the reason why sadly we cannot claim to have anything like the best fans in the country.

So, you're a season ticket holder and go to a few away games, you never bother with cup games, does this mean your a shit supporter? The way a few are speaking, it sounds like it.

In between such antics the aforementioned cup final ticket allocation arose – another bitching session, one of panic and/or justification regarding whether or not you deserve a ticket for the final.

Yesterday's attendance was poor and I believe that anyone there should be guaranteed a ticket for the final (and I was not there). I didn't go because I simply could not be arsed with the drive and expense for a game on television. Around six years ago I cannot imagine I would ever have missed a game through apathy but personally I feel I have been let down one too many times by the Club and Murray in particular.

I think if you have a season ticket and go to away games but never bother with cup tickets you could say you would deserve to go to the play off final for instance, but you shouldn't take the place of someone who had been to all the early rounds if we got to the cup final!

Absolute total bollocks, a season ticket holder shouldn't be entitled to a final ticket despite shelling out over £300 up front but a bloke who has been to three or four games should? Think again.

And the argument went on into the early hours. What's ironic about this piece is that you could cut and paste it into any book about any football club, not just Sunderland AFC. I wonder though, how many of those pissed off fans who were told to go and support the Mags, actually did and that is the reason the Skunks have attendances of over fifty thousand every other week? Have the *'high and mighty'* driven away genuine supporters with genuine feelings who fail to abide by their military dictatorship and have indeed fucked off to support those up the road – interesting theory I think.

XVI

"What really riles the Geordies is that we lost and still went up!"

Tommy Smith's two goals against Birmingham City in the F. A. Cup replay put SAFC into the quarter–finals, and the first time we had appeared in the F. A. Cup quarter finals since the last time! It set–up a winnable tie against Sheffield United at the Stadium of Light, and a game where the atmosphere, the tension, the passion, and the spark was put back into supporting the Lads, not just for me, but for thousands of others as well. I hadn't been to too many games, those I had been to had ended up being run of the mill encounters with little to no passion visible from the committed that had turned out. The home game against Palace didn't spark until Marcus Stewart's last minute penalty winner. What followed was a round of unimpressive goalless draws – Cardiff City (I went to this game solely to do some research for another book I'm writing about hooliganism, and although a nasty fracas did occur, I, in my astute wisdom knew nothing about it); Rotherham United, Coventry City, and the dull win over Wimbledon. Bar the game against the Monkey Hangers, the choice of games I was attending were bad ones at that (though they did pick up – home games against West Ham, Derby County, Sheffield United being games more like what games at home should be like). The Quarter Final however was completely different. The atmosphere was electric, the game pulsating. A move initiated by Julio Arca to George McCartney set up Tommy Smith who fired home a left foot shot into the corner of the net. Get in, one up after less than ten minutes. United, playing with boo–boy favourite Ashley Ward, were a handful, but the Sunderland goal along with Ward being substituted in the first half following a clash with *'bruiser'* Kevin Kyle, subdued them for a while – the Stadium of Light is no happy hunting ground for Ashley Ward (shame).

First half, it was more or less all Sunderland, second half as expected, the Blades came out firing, having made a double substitution, and it turned into a nerve–wracking encounter, more so when Arca was stretchered off after seventy five minutes (and would hardly play again for Sunderland for the remainder of the season). Sunderland, however, hung on. Stephen Wright was an inspiration, even Phil Babb played well as the Sunderland defence kept a clean sheet, steering the team into the semi–finals. Fuck me, this team, the Club, the events of the past twelve months and suddenly we were ninety minutes away from a cup final. I doubt supporting any other team could produce so many twists and turns. The Cup suddenly became the focus of everything, and led to that old chestnut of Cup or promotion. Why not both though? I left the Stadium after that match quite proud and excited. It certainly had boosted my allegiance. I was no longer a fan that blows hot and cold, I was a supporter who supports, and I decided that renewing my season ticket was to be a priority for 2004–2005 and I'd renew regardless of the outcome of the Cup and the push for the Premiership. *Why Do I Do It?* had started and ended with relegation. This book may have started with the demise of Sunderland from the top flight, carrying on from where *Why Do I Do It?* left off, but at this rate it would hopefully end with tears of joy and possibly some major silverware. Sunderland were of course holders of the record of being the last team in the North east to win a major trophy – 1973, however The Smoggies had taken that record off us recently by winning the League Cup. That was our crown they had stolen. Hopefully however we'd be getting it back within a few weeks!

XVII

"I wear my cap backwards 'cos I'm git cool!"

Cup fever! Once every so many years we get it. Some teams get it every year. Some teams never get it. For Sunderland, cup fever had hit for the first time in over a decade. The tension was building as the draw for the semi-final loomed. Walking home from the quarter final, the pros and cons of the remaining teams were weighed up in my mind. If it was Arsenal, we may just be able to claim a shock win – we had beaten Arsenal in the semis in '73 – destiny beckoned! Then again we'd probably get thrashed. Did it therefore mean it'd be better to be thrashed in the semi than the final? If we drew Manchester United then likewise we had a good chance of winning, more so than Arsenal, seeing as United's form was, with respect to their reputation, fucking disgraceful. That left the draw pitting us against the winners of the Millwall versus Tranmere replay – Millwall, a fellow Division One side who had done the double on us, or Tranmere Rovers, forever a thorn in our side.

The venue was pretty obvious too – a game against Manchester United would mean a trip to Villa Park, Arsenal a trip to Old Trafford. Prior to the draw being made, I discovered that if we reached the final we'd be guaranteed European football, due to the imminent re-qualification of Man. Utd and Arsenal into the Champions League. With that in mind the semi-final would effectively be our final. SAFC were therefore ninety minutes away from wiping whatever alleged debt they had in recent seasons accumulated.

The draw was made. Sunderland were first out of the hat and drawn against ... Millwall or Tranmere Rovers. And so a lower league side was guaranteed to be playing in the final (then again if we were promoted it wouldn't, as we'd be a Premiership team once more).

Calls of fix, fix, fix could be heard being mumbled all around. But regardless of how the balls came out the term fix would've been made. If the two big boys had been kept apart it would've been fixed to guarantee two *'giants'* in the final and satisfy a world wide audience wanting to watch England's show piece game take place between the so-called *'best in the land.'* If on the other hand they were drawn together it'd be a fix to ensure the glamour and the romance of the FA Cup was intact by having an underdog, and therefore a David and Goliath clash in the final.

The fact of the matter was that we got the best possible draw. We were now within ninety minutes of the UEFA Cup and ninety minutes of a Cardiff final, and the first lower league team to reach the final in twelve years – and back then in '92 that team was us!

Bob Stokoe was definitely shining down on SAFC. The gloom of the previous season was well and truly on its way to being vanquished forever. However the gloom was hitting me. I had refused to renew my season ticket on the grounds of disgust at a bunch if mercenaries, a bunch of inept executives, a club that had personally intimidated me, and as a result of not renewing, panic struck. How would I get a ticket for the semi?

The day after the draw, ticket details were announced by the Club, for season tickets holders only at this stage, who had first choice, which is always the case and rightly so. After that the Club would offer remaining tickets to those with the biggest number of loyalty points – in other words games attended over the course of the season. If however you had paid on the day at the turnstiles then such attendances would not count. You could therefore have a scenario of people having been to every home game but would not be offered a semi-final ticket. Unfair? Yes and no. The thing is at times like this there's always a panic to get tickets. Clubs try their best to offer the precious gold dust in the fairest of ways. There are always those who miss out undeservedly and those who obtain tickets undeservedly. It appears that at times like this the *"I'm a better fan than you"* arguments are resurrected, supporters hoping they get a ticket and praying others don't. Bickering and fighting always happens when a scramble takes place, and fans come crawling out of the woodwork declaring themselves to be loyal and deserving.

What didn't help in SAFC's situation was the way in which the announcement of tickets being sold was made. SAFC were rewarding *'their'* loyal fans.

Now hang on a minute what exactly is a *'loyal'* fan?

I had had a season ticket for over ten years (actually since I struggled to get tickets for the '92 semi-final and final, and after attending all home games and a half dozen or more away games that season).

I had not renewed this season.

My record was thus ten for and one against and as such the semi-final ticket announcement could be literally read as saying that I was no longer loyal.

I believe that there's a time and a place to put across supporters as being loyal. This wasn't and in my opinion a rather pedantic and pretentious press release was announced, which was followed with a subtle hint that loyalty points for games attended would also include forthcoming matches. The day after this press release was put out, we played Present North End at home – subtle hint my arse.

I had only attended four games for the entire season that could be tracked. The remaining games I had gone to were paid for in cash on the turnstiles. I was skint. Tickets for the semi were in the region of £55. I couldn't afford to go to the Preston game, and the semi final (as well as other games leading up to the Old Trafford tie). Upping my loyalty level to five recorded games wouldn't put me any higher up on the reward ladder as far as I was concerned.

The only way to get a ticket would by via those you know or paying over the top to a tout. Still, even though I didn't stand much chance of getting a ticket, I still booked myself onto a coach down to Old Trafford.

I decided to stop worrying and wait until the official announcement of exact allocated numbers was made and how they'd go on sale to the general public before worrying further. I did however join a gym, mainly to toughen up for the scrimmage that would inevitably take place – the fee for all brawls to get your hand on Willy Wonka's *'golden ticket.'*

After the 3-3 draw against Preston the non–season ticket holder semi–final availability was made public. You only needed to have attended three games to qualify, but apparently league games only and home ones at that. Bollocks. I should have gone to Preston.

That would've topped me up to three; cup games just didn't count. Then again all I had to do was phone up the ticket office and buy three tickets for the next three home games. Ah but I was skint so I couldn't. Maybe when I was younger and a bit more carefree I would have found the money, but times change, attitudes and priorities change.

The press release about general sale really did put the final nail in the coffin as far as I could see when it came to actually getting a ticket. Then again, if say I had enough points already, or if I had bought tickets for the next three home games, it still did not guarantee a ticket.

The minimum tally required meant you'd be put in a hat and a lottery style draw would take place to determine who got a ticket for Old Trafford.

Hmmm, that meant spending over £60 to stand a chance of having to fork out somewhere in the region of what would probably be £100 for the whole semi-final experience (ticket, transport, refreshments etc).

Attendances for the following three home games did not dramatically increase thus the con of forking out hadn't paid off. SAFC then put out another lottery – the general-general sale for those classed as being way down in the loyalty pecking order – *'The Barrel Scrapers'*, which meant me. So off went a stamped addressed envelope in the hope!

I'd now applied myself, had season ticket holders I knew apply for extra tickets for me, had contacted people in the media and certain supporter's branches for any possible spares they might have, and had even managed to apply for a press pass – something which was quite an achievement to be honest.

I tried contacting Old Trafford initially via email, enquiring about obtaining a press pass. I wasn't ignored like you'd expect from say the likes of SAFC, but was told to telephone, which I didn't fancy doing just yet.

An official press release from SAFC themselves to the media in general advising them of the procedure required to apply for a press pass came winging my way – not direct from SAFC, but from a reliable source officially classed as media rather than me, officially classed as a tosser!

The email advised all applications to be made via fax on letter headed paper, and so I copied the RTG logo into Microsoft Word and wrote out my blag, full of porkies (yes and no, well probably more yes than no).

17th March 2003

Dear Sir/Madam,

I wish to apply for one press pass for the F. A. Cup Semi-Final at Old Trafford having been provided this fax number via the press release issued by SAFC on 16th March 2003 **[somewhat illegally passed onto me however].**
I am one of two editors for www.readytogo.net (Ready To Go), the independent web site 'fanzine' for Sunderland AFC supporters. Ready To Go offers SAFC fans worldwide

the opportunity to communicate with each other via one of the biggest online forums in the UK **[though a self-proclaimed title]**, *has regular news feeds, news updates, and match reports, and has been providing this service since 1997 (average monthly page views in excess of 18,000,000)* **[ouch that's a big porky as RTG pulls roughly half of that]**. *I wish to continue my reporting as I have done at previous grounds in the past* **[but I never have]** *and offer a more detailed account of the day's proceedings on this historic occasion for SAFC.*

I am also an author developing a number of books this year and have produced one of the most successful fan based books in recent years and the number one best selling local paperback in Sunderland **[now that's not a lie – honest]** *for Xmas 2003 (Why Do I Do It? – www.whydoidoit.co.uk).*

The match report I wish to produce will form part of the ongoing service provided by Ready To Go and the basis for my next book (a follow–up to last Xmas' hit).

Ready To Go is an online Internet company (partnership) primarily devoting its time to SAFC. If my application is successful, then blah blah blah blah blah blah blah blah blah blah blah blah blah **[and so on – well there's no need to go on and on and on and on and re–print every bum licking sentence I put together]**.

I did carefully think through what I wrote, and even though I hastily put it together, and even though it smelled of *'BS'*, I decided if I could venture into the press box at Old Trafford then it would make for a great chapter in this book, thus the reason to mention my exploits into the world of novel writing.

At the same time however I would take my laptop and digital camera and provided a telephone line was available I intended on relaying updates live on the web for those unfortunate souls unable to watch the game.

Fair enough, the tales of RTG's success was exaggerated, but I was honest with my intentions regarding the book.

I guess mixing fact with fiction is what helped me win through in the end as I received an email from Old Trafford three days later stating words along the lines of:

20ᵗʰ *March 2004*

Dear Mr. Han,

Thank you for your recent press application for the forthcoming F. A. Cup Semi-Final taking place at Old Trafford. A ticket will be available for you to collect from the press entrance on Sunday 4ᵗʰ April 2004.

Shit! I had pulled off one major blag and now had free entry into Old Trafford – for the F. A. Cup Semi Final. Fucking hell! You may or may not have seen the MTV show actually called *'Blag'*, well this one is/was worthy of appearing on there. However, I reluctantly turned down the press pass. The idea of mixing it with the media was intriguing and would have made for a great chapter, but I was worried that SAFC, renowned for trying to expel fanzine representatives at certain matches, would question who I was and I'd be booted out, leaving me ticket-less outside of Old Trafford, while inside Sunderland stormed to victory, and Europe, never mind the final. Besides it would also mean I'd have to dress sensibly, not being able to wear my colours and would also mean I'd have to behave – and not jump around like a loon when SAFC scored.

The ease at which I blagged a press pass however was quite remarkable. I doubt the applications were being vetted by SAFC, otherwise I wouldn't have received one, but it's quite easy when you think about it to actually apply and more importantly, be successful. All you have to do it put together a web site that looks impressive – a few pages would suffice, get a cheap domain name which these days cost around a tenner and seeing as web addresses are put live within forty eight hours, and that free web space is readily available on the Internet, the impression one can give is that of being some multi-national consortium. At the end of the day all they would say is no, but for a tenner it's worth the try – and cheaper than buying three tickets in advance from SAFC in their quick buck money making scheme forcing fans desperate to see the semi-final to fork out sixty odd quid in the hope of receiving a ticket.

However regardless of how interesting a chapter it would have made, I declined it mainly due to getting an actual match ticket. In fact every route I'd chosen, every path I'd followed in my quest to get a ticket, came up trumps. First off a ticket arrived at my home address, followed by two tickets arriving at RTG's P. O. Box address and the SAFCSA Jarrow Branch had two tickets spare. All I wanted was one and now I had six including the press pass! The Jarrow Branch tickets had initially came to me through Neil A - the Cable Guy, or rather Alien as he is fondly known as (being Neil A backwards). With guilt still ridden inside me from not getting him a ticket for the Charlton play-off final I decided to take up the offer of tickets with him and pay for them both, my way of making up with him and reward for his proof-reading efforts in sorting out my bad spelling, grammar and punctuation in all of my literary efforts to date. As for the other tickets, well I could have made a packet selling them for profit, my RTG colleague sold the two tickets that had arrived via our P O Box (for face value), and I sold the one that had arrived at my address (for face value) - yes I could have made a small fortune but I didn't, I'm not in the game of exploiting SAFC supporters, for fuck's sake I've been running a free web site since 1997 - proof if you ever needed it that I don't charge for my services! I put out an advert on the SMB, a first come first served notice of a ticket for sale. The first reply I had was from a lad known as 'Rex', (Mark) who thankful for finally getting hold of a ticket, offered me a lift, so I ended up travelling with him to the game. Strange how panic had set in, regret over not renewing my season ticket and not being instantly guaranteed a ticket, and yet with word of mouth, a bit of advertising and a cleverly construed blag, I ended up with more than I needed, but the excess wasn't wasted, well maybe the press pass, but the extra tickets went to fellow supporters who initially, like me thought they'd never be able to go to Old Trafford. Now however they could undertake a pilgrimage to the so-called 'Theatre Of Dreams' and what had to be certain glory.

XVIII

"I agree wholeheartedly with the comments made by the person below!"

With the semi-final showdown fast approaching, the Soothsayers and superstitious paranoid lunatics were rising high, predicting victory, and laying down their mumbo-jumbo and formulated theories as to why SAFC would not only win the semi-final, but actually win the cup. Some of the theories presented were indeed spooky; others were clinging onto the proverbial thread of hope. Still it showed a mass of people excited about the entire prospect and something to make even the most disillusioned SAFC fan smile – does that mean me?

Lucky colours, lucky names, lucky coincidences, lucky teams, lucky, lucky, lucky-luck reasons were banded about, and for some reason it appeared that these old wives' tales would determine the outcome of SAFC rather than any football being played!

So what was being presented and amalgamated?

Well Scottish football club Hibernian provided one such *'we will win because...'* theory. Bob Stokoe and the number 73 provided another theory. The number 20, the number 4, the number 7, the letter S, Mart Poom, Jimmy Montgomery, fourth round ties, and the colour green were just a few of the many differing and colourful explanations that were doing the rounds.

Hibernian

In 1973 Hibs lost the Scottish league cup final, but in 1992 Hibs won Scottish league cup final. In 2004 Hibs lost Scottish league cup final. Sunderland on the other hand won the F. A. Cup in 1973, lost the F. A. Cup in 1992 and, well, it was 2004. The other defining factor regarding Hibs is that the first letter of the teams we'd played up to the semi final (Hartlepool United, Ipswich

Town, Birmingham City and Sheffield United), spelled out HIBS.

The Number 20

Sunderland won the F. A. Cup in 1937. By adding all the digits of the year 1937 together you get 20. We also won the F. A. Cup in 1973, and by adding all the digits of the year 1973 together you get the number 20. It was now 2004. Adding the numbers together you get 6. However if SAFC were to win the Cup, we'd have won it three times and therefore 6X3 = 18 which if added to how many times we've lost the cup – twice – you get the number 20. Thomas Butler wore the number twenty and was 20 to 1 to score in the final should he be named in a squad of 20! Gamblers were therefore insisting a bet of twenty quid was a must.

The Number 4

Sunderland won the F. A. Cup in 1937, 1973 and would hopefully do so again in 2004. The magic number is four if you apply the following formula.

1937. 7–3 = 4 (a reverse of the numbers as it was in the 70's)
1973. 7–3 = 4
2004. 4–0 = 4.

There's 4 letters in HIBS. There's 4 letters in SAFC. There's 4 letters in Kyle – a potential match winner! The winner of the 2004 Grand National was allocated the number 17 – two digits, add them together and divide by the number of digits (1+7 / 2 = 4). Since winning the F. A. Cup in 1973, thirty–one years have past, thus 3+1 = 4 . Or take the following years and subtract them from each other – 2004–1937= 67 ((6+7) = 13, (1+3) = 4). The semi final date – the 4th of April 2004 thus 04/04/04 and the kick–off time scheduled for 13.00 hours means 1+3 = 4. Winning the semi–final would mean 4 wins in a row for SAFC. Club captain Jason McAteer wore number 4 and had played in three cup ties leading up to the semi final. Surely his influence and experience would lead SAFC onto glory in what would be his fourth cup–tie appearance for the season. Since beating Liverpool at Anfield in 1960/61 Sunderland had won away ties in the fourth round on only three occasions. In 1973, while playing in the second tier of English football, they won a 4th round replay at Elm Park, Reading and went on to win the Cup. In 1992, while playing in the second tier of English football, they won at Oxford's Manor Ground and went on to reach the final. And in 2004, while playing in the second tier of English football, they won at Portman Road, Ipswich, and went on to...

The Letter S

The name Sunderland begins with a letter S, and in 1937 began with the letter S. Unbelievably, again in 1973 it began with the letter S, and what do you know, here we were in 2004, and yes, Sunderland still began with the letter S. Tommy Smith was also SAFC's leading scorer in the F. A. Cup and his surname begins with an S, as does the surname of 'The Messiah' Bob Stokoe who was manager when Sunderland won the cup in 1973 and who sadly passed away in 2004.

The Number 7

Pretty obvious is the number 7 as the digit appears in the years 1973, and 1937. Bob Stokoe died on February 1st 2004 which if added together from the date format of 01–02–04 you get the number 7. We reached the semi final by defeating Sheffield United on March 7th whilst lying 7th in Division One. Sunderland was also the 7th team to qualify for the F. A. Cup quarter–finals, and have appeared in 7 Wembley finals (1913, 1937, 1973, 1985, 1990, 1992, 1998).

[Authors note: I can relate to the number 7 seeing as I was born in 1967; my birthday is the 17th, my wife's birthday is the 17th, my youngest daughter's birthday is the 7th and my fathers birthday is the 17th].

Mart Poom & Jimmy Montgomery

If you take the initial letter from the surname of our last winning goalie (Jimmy Montgomery), and the first from the forename of our current goalie (Mart Poom), and you get MM. Our current Manager's initials – Mick McCarthy.

The Bible Code

There is a binary pattern that runs through the books of Deuteronomy and Leviticus that quite clearly stated Sunderland would win the cup in 2004.

War & Peace

By applying the mathematical formula of $Y = 1973Ln(x) - 2004(R^n)\ 4b\ /\ (7*20)$ which basically refers to Y as the defining logical parameter for concluding the analytic cogitation of $1973Ln(x)$; Ln the linear path or timeline of the history of the F. A. Cup competition, (x) as the secret ingredient *'chemical x'* (stolen from The Power Puff Girls), 2004 being the current year (R^n) being the infinite value of the absolute geometric reflective parabola radius of inversion, 4b relating to the quadratic average from dividing the current sub–total against seven times twenty. The answer becomes a randomised skip code not too dissimilar to the Bible Code and when applied to War & Peace by Leo Tolstoy, it just so happens to coincide with chapter seventy–three (I hope the following isn't copyrighted):

> *"Well begin!" said Dolokhov. "All right," said Pierre, still smiling in the same way. A feeling of dread was in the air. It was evident that the affair so lightly begun could no longer be averted but was taking its course independently of men's will. Denisov first went to the barrier and announced: "As the adve'sawies have wefused a weconciliation, please pwoceed. Take your pistols, and at the word thwee begin to*

advance. "O–ne! T–wo! Thwee!" he shouted angrily and stepped aside. The combatants advanced along the trodden tracks, nearer and nearer to one another, beginning to see one another through the mist. They had the right to fire when they liked as they approached the barrier. Dolokhov walked slowly without raising his pistol, looking intently with his bright, sparkling blue eyes into his antagonist's face. His mouth wore its usual semblance of a smile.

"So I can fire when I like!" said Pierre, and at the word three," he went quickly forward, missing the trodden path and stepping into the deep snow. He held the pistol in his right hand at arm's length, apparently afraid of shooting himself with it. His left hand he held carefully back, because he wished to support his right hand with it and knew he must not do so. Having advanced six paces and strayed off the track into the snow, Pierre looked down at his feet, then quickly glanced at Dolokhov and, bending his finger as he had been shown, fired. Not at all expecting so loud a report, Pierre shuddered at the sound and then, smiling at his own sensations, stood still. The smoke, rendered denser by the mist, prevented him from seeing anything for an instant, but there was no second report as he had expected. He only heard Dolokhov's hurried steps, and his figure came in view through the smoke. He was pressing one hand to his left side, while the other clutched his drooping pistol. His face was pale. Rostov ran toward him and said something.

This skip code when correctly spaced out reads **sunderland f a cup two thousand and four.**

The Colour Green

My own superstition has always been to wear my colours – stripes – at all home games. I guess that's not too much of a superstition to have, but seeing as I started to eat all the pies, my top no longer fitted and so I stopped wearing colours to any game I actually bothered to go and watch.

At the Hartlepool third round tie I wore a green long sleeved t-shirt and likewise wore it while shopping in the

Bridges on the day we played Ipswich. I also wore it while watching the Birmingham game on telly, and also had the same t-shirt on for work when the Birmingham replay took place.

I decided therefore to wear it for the Sheffield United game. Basically dared not wear it for the semi and (hopefully at the time of writing) the final.

XIX

"ATTACK, ATTACK, ATTACK –
I loved that Roker End scoreboard!"

Old Trafford isn't all that impressive you know. Well it isn't too me. Outside there's an interesting array of stands, walls glassed up with statues scattered about the place and what have you. Semi-Final day in Manchester was dry but windy. In fact it was so windy a few Man. United officials were desperately trying to glue down the hairpiece (a Mexican wave) from Bobby Charlton's statue!

The last time I was at Old Trafford, The Lads drew 2-2 in the F. A. Cup third round, goals from Craig Russell and Steve Agnew. Back then the approach and surrounding area was one large, dirty, and an extremely run down looking industrial wasteland. Since then the area really has been tarted-up, with business parks, fancy hotels, city centre access points, and the impressive looking Trafford Shopping Centre.

Getting to Old Trafford early meant a long, long wait before Alien turned up to collect the ticket I was holding for him and I'll tell you what, I could have made a packet out of touting it. Ordinary fans without tickets wandered around aimlessly, "Got any spare tickets", touts were obvious to spot, and making a killing out of those without an *'entry pass'*. Alien's ticket could've been sold tenfold before he turned up, but such thoughts never entered my mind as I roamed around for a while spotting a few people I knew and soaking up the atmosphere, which is quite strange when you're sober. Close to the East Stand I grabbed some van food in and amongst the Millwall fans, the majority of whom, fully coloured–up, were keeping themselves to themselves and, much like the hoards of Mackems waiting for the turnstiles to open, were polite, and friendly. However, there's always one, and me being a shit magnet, they always focus their attention for some fucking annoying reason on me. A pissed–up short-arsed Cockney bastard with a Lions flag draped around his shoulders was trying to beef up the atmosphere obviously intent on making it a more hostile one rather than a friendly one.

No One likes us,
No one likes us,
No one likes us,
We Don't Care,
We are Millwall,
Super Millwall,
We are Millwall
From The Den.

He may have been *'Millwall'* but the rest of his fellow supporters were simply ignoring him and simply *'didn't care'*. He wandered around singing his one line song over and over again, and then he made eye contact with me and started strolling over.

"Cam on 'en far–king join in wiya. We are Millwall, no one like us..." I stepped to one side.

"Wassa marra, far–king cat got yer tongue."

"No mate," I replied (though he wasn't my mate), "I'm a Mackem."

"Oh fark–king Norvena eh, no calas facking casual eh? Let's ave it then."

I turned and walked away – briskly yes, but hey I'm no thug nor did I want to *'ave it'* – especially before the bloody game had kicked off though I have to say that I am not the type

113

to go looking for *'it'* after a game either. Yeah I was dressed all *'casual'* but that was due to superstition.

I headed off down towards the West Stand (the Stretford End) and the Sunderland area through a dark tunnel with entrances that looked more like airport terminal access points than turnstiles or executive lobbies.

I have to mention here that the press entrance was down this way, but upon approaching it, I felt no concern or regret for giving up the press pass I had managed to blag. As I walked passed Messrs Rowell and Crabtree were outside waiting to get in. I have to mention Crabbers you see as he gets a little paranoid now and then – he never got a mention in the first edition of *Why Do I Do It?* I guess I've made up for it now right Simon?

After a few text messages and phone calls, Alien was within fifteen minutes of the ground on the SAFC London Branch bus he was travelling up in, so I found a spot for us to meet, next to where the Sunderland team coach had parked, and waited, thirsty, and anxious. A young girl brushed past me. She apologised for she was ever so excited due to a bottle of water she was holding that Sean Thornton had had on the coach and had given to her upon getting off (young girls and their affection towards players – how sweet).

My phone rang. It was Alien he was standing next to a red coach and couldn't see me. I looked to my right and there he was. Fucking hell it had been about six years since we'd last seen each other and here we were standing ten feet apart and didn't recognise each other. I handed over the precious golden ticket and off into the ground it was. Then again, was it a football ground? Once through the turnstiles, the path leading up towards the top half of the Stretford End (a caged–in set of stairs), resembled what looked more like those you queue up in to go on some fancy theme park ride. Three hours later most Mackems had reached the summit, exhausted, thirsty, and a clever move by Manchester United – headed towards to crowded kiosks to buy unique two pint plastic cups of larger. Well you needed one that big having climbed the UK's equivalent of a Mount Everest sized stadium.

The view was great, though the ground looked small, and what hit me more than anything else was the mass of empty seats in the upper tier of the section Millwall were housed in. In fact there were ten thousand empty seats. How many Mackems would have loved to get hold of tickets for there? The F. A. fucked up big time on ticket allocation if ask me. It was a damn disgrace that so many seats were allowed to remain empty. For fuck's sake Millwall's average gate was around 14,000 so why give them thirty odd thousand? SAFC could have sold 50,000 easily, but that's part and parcel of both semi-finals and finals, the *under-allocation*, the scramble, fighting, and stress involved in order just to get a ticket.

One thing I noticed when I walked out onto the *terracing*, was just how alarmingly steep the upper tiers of the Stretford End were. A number of web sites carried a report stating that fans sitting at the front of Manchester United's Stretford End could face the risk of a catastrophic accident taking place due to the possibility of fans falling over the edge of the second tier because barriers currently in place were not designed to hold back a standing spectator (and as we all know when a goal is scored one would naturally stand up).

Well that explained the reason why the stewards were frantically running up and down the stairs asking people to sit down. Without a doubt if Sunderland had scored someone at the back could have jumped up, fallen forward, and started a dangerous domino effect of spiralling bodies heading toward the front and disaster – thank God we didn't score then, eh?

And so the game kicked off. This was it. This was our final. Winning meant a pot of gold and qualification for the UEFA Cup. This was Millwall we were playing. We could beat a shit team like this, couldn't we?

Reaching the final would mean a nice day out, without a care in the world whether we won or not, the European dream would by then be a reality.

No one wanted Millwall in Europe, not with the reputation their fans have.

If ever a game of football was to be fixed, this was it.

The F A wanted us to win.

UEFA wanted us to win.

Sepp Blatter wanted us to win.

Christ, even Tony Blair wanted us to win.

As usual our leading goal scorer was on the bench, our most creative midfielder was on the bench and our hardest midfielder, a player you wanted on the park to control the ankle biter known as Dennis Wise was suspended (Marcus Stewart, Sean Thornton, and Jeff Whitley respectively).

Something was a-foot. This was a semi-final and we always win semi-finals – in my lifetime at least – but this was to all intents and purposes our final, and we always bottle it when it comes to the big crunch *'all or nothing'* games. In recent times, Sunderland AFC have become perennial chokers – Play Off Final 1998, F. A. Cup Final 1992, Milk Cup Final 1985, Play Off Final 1990, relegation crunch time 1996, relegation crunch time 1991, Europe or bust (or so they said) in 2002, relegation in 2004 (season long chokers), and now the FA Cup Semi Final 2004.

Full time, Millwall 1 Sunderland 0, a soft goal, a fluff, a fuck-up by George McCartney and Phil Babb, but once tagged as either a popular player or an unpopular player, the tag sticks. McCartney is popular and so Babb got the blame. Midfield wise we were shocking. Paul Thirlwell – why oh why was he playing? What did he do? Nowt. And as the song goes,

Oh he loves to pass it to the left side,
Oh he loves to pass it to the right,
Oh he loves to play it like a crab, crab, crab,
That's because Paul Bracewell [allegedly] *is his dad, dad, dad.*

Paul, Paul, Paul, I really, really, really hated you that day, you were a crab, you were a Cyclops, your vision was null, and you bottled it. You made sure you were a minimum safe distance from Dennis Wise.

As such we played the semi-final with ten men!

In fact I don't think Thirlwell knew what he was doing on the pitch. I'm not meaning this to be a personal attack but what was it with all the finger pointing he was doing?

At times he reminded me of Homer Simpson and how his attention span or lack of it gets to him and inside his head he is merrily humming away to some annoying tune like "The Birdie Song" -

Der, der, der, dah, der, dah, der,
Der, dah, der, dah, der, dah, der,
Dah, dah, dah, dah, bom, bom, bom bom,

- while all around him, chaos reigns. And now I've managed through the power of suggestion to place "The Birdie Song" into your head and I guarantee when you've finished, this page or chapter, or session of reading, "The Birdie Song" will still be there being hummed by your sub-conscious, buried deep within in your cerebral mass.

When you retire tonight and lie in total darkness and total silence slowly drifting off to sleep, "The Birdie Song" will pop back into your head. Annoying, isn't it? That's Paul Thirlwell to me - annoying (and I'm holding back and being as polite as I can here).

As for other players, well *'alleged'* Club captain Jason *'Jemma Jaimeson'* McAteer, was an embarrassment, getting sent off for some foolish tackles and overall had a fucking pathetic game.

We were now playing the semi-final with nine men!

We tried, boy did we try. But, we failed. Kevin Kyle oh so quiet throughout the first half, started in the second half to show more bite and was clearly beginning to cause the Millwall back four problems. Mick McCarthy therefore took him off!

It could have been so different. We were just not up for it, we did not play our strongest team and we lost. Millions were poured down the drain. The Club's share price probably plummeted. Uncle Bob - so near and yet so far again - when will you stand up and be counted - walk away please?

117

Another game where the words 'if' and 'only' became the topic of conversation for days after. 'If only' John Oster's fee kick had bounced on the right side of the goal line after hitting the underside of the crossbar (after only five minutes). But it wasn't to be. You think we'd have learned to get used to being let down. Each time it happens it hurts as if it was the first time it had ever happened.

I was upset and angry. I could not believe how so many players upon full lime legged it off the pitch. What happened to showing your disappointment with us fans? Marcus Stewart, Mart Poom, Sean Thornton, and Julio Arca were the only ones I spotted who did remain on the pitch to share in the disappointment of losing. Arca slumped to the floor in a pool of tears. I just shrugged my shoulders, said my farewells to Alien and left the ground.

The green top superstition hadn't worked. In fact had any of the superstitions worked? If Bob Stokoe was shining down on us, he must have blinked or was too busy with other commitments – maybe a lunch break with Raich Carter and Dave Halliday.

Later however the superstition surrounding the number four stood up, took a deep breath and laughed in our faces. Jason McAteer was sent off – number four, Tim Cahill scored the winner for Millwall – and was wearing number four. That was it. Fuck superstition, it's pointless and it hurts when it fails (oh and let's not forget the curse of the Manager of the Month award – Mick McCarthy winning the title for the First Division a few days prior to the semi-final).

I went to the toilet before leaving Old Trafford but by the time I'd descended the death trap exit route I was bursting again. Thankfully there was a pub close to where the car was parked so I could relieve myself before grabbing some more van food. As I entered the car park, tying to remember what the car I'd got a lift down in with Rex, the lad I'd sold a spare ticket too looked like, a voice behind me shouted "Oi Sanlan". I turned around and it was that fucking 'We Don't Care' Millwall supporter that had had a go at me before the game. Shit. How the fuck had he managed to find me? Had he gone looking for me or was this really a case of being in the wrong place at the wrong time?

He started walking over towards me singing the one and only song he and probably every other Millwall fan would endlessly sing;

No One likes us,
No one likes us,
No one likes us,
We Don't Care,
We are Millwall,
Super Millwall,
We are Millwall from The Den.

I wanted to leg it to the car, but panic was setting in and I just froze. He had materialised from nowhere and was in my face before I knew it.

"Cam on 'en you far-king cahnt, lets ave it. Far-king Sanlan, you far-king Seaburn. Look at ya wiya fancy Stown Islan' jacket an' woz 'em eh, far-king Front Shoes, you far-king wan' some, I far-king wan' some".

Shit I wasn't wearing my colours so in his eyes I was a hooligan.

He was calling me Seaburn.

Fuck, he thought I was a Seaburn Casual.

If he knew the name of Sunderland's *'notorious'* firm then there was a good chance he was a Millwall *'Bushwacker'*.

He was also pissed, well and truly pissed.

I wasn't wearing any Stone Island gear. Fucking hell I've got a wife and two kids. Why would I buy a jacket that cost two hundred fucking quid? My casual style was fucking Matalan and George not fucking Burberry, Aquascutum, Paul & Shark, or whatever designer clobber normally associated with hooligans.

His face was so close to mine he was practically kissing me. His breath fucking stunk and I had no idea what to do. My heart was racing. I was panic-stricken. No one else was around. I couldn't see the car, nor see Rex anywhere either. I'd just left a ground containing over fifty thousand people and yet here I was alone with a thug. Millwall wanted my blood, he wouldn't let it lie. "Far–king cam on 'en let's ave it".

Queue Ennio Morricone's theme from *"The Good, The Bad, And The Ugly"*. I am of course the man with no name. The hood on my jacket flapped up over my head silhouetting my face, much like Clint Eastwood's. I was frowning, my hotdog was my cigar, my eyes were squinting, staring at Millwall, the bad guy, the drunken thug, who was about to draw first. I was shitting myself, I couldn't move, the fear, so intense, yet so exciting.

Does that make sense?

I knew I have to defend myself and maybe, just maybe I think to myself, this drunken arsehole in front of me might be a tad slow and I might able me to get the fuck out of his way, or pray Rex arrived as back-up, well before any of Millwall's mates turned up, in which case – P D Han – R.I.P.

My legs suddenly kicked in and I was moving, slowly at first, backing away – cautiously and hopefully towards the car, somewhere behind me (I dared not turn around and look, I had to keep eye contact with Millwall, watching to counteract whatever move he was going to make).

"Far–king cam on 'en".

He nudged me by pushing his forehead against mine.

"Look" I said, "I want no trouble, you won today, just err go off and err celebrate alright?"

"I am far–king celebwating in eye?"

His brow was still touching mine. He was screaming down my throat and I sensed that he was preparing to make his final, and I feared, fatal blow.

Within an instant he was on the floor crying like a bairn, dazed with blood pouring from his nose. I never knew I had it in me, but I had somehow lobbed my head back and hit him as hard as I could.

Bulls–eye!

I landed full force onto his nose sending him sprawling to the ground. "Ahhh you far–king cahnt you've far–king browk my far–king nose".

"Fuck you", I said.

"I told you I wanted no trouble".

"Far–king cahnt. Far–king cahnt".

As he lay there some prehistoric Neanderthal instinct must have taken over me as I lashed into him kicking him hard in the stomach. "Fuck you," I said again turning to see a shocked Rex, already in the car, engine running, desperately signalling for me to get in. I did, and he drove off rather quickly. He never talked about it, nor did I want to discuss what had just happened. As far as I'm concerned, it was self–defence.

I'm not a thug. I don't go looking for trouble. Trouble had come to me, trouble had decided I was fair game, but trouble had ended up in trouble.

Fucking Cockney wanker.

What had I done to deserve this? How the hell had he managed to find me?

As we drove back up to Sunderland, my head was thumping, I could feel a migraine coming on, and I had a nasty red mark from where I'd nutted him.

So fucking what!

SAFC had lost the F. A. Cup semi–final, but yet I was more upset that I had been in a fight with a rival footy fan.

I am not a hooligan you know.

I'm only five foot, six inches.

Just 'cos my ASDA coat looked like some fancy hoolie gear didn't warrant some obvious hooligan wanting to butt–fuck me. He was pissed and thankfully that, I assume, saved me from a good beating. His balance was weak and so I easily managed to floor him.

Served him right.

This really was the icing on the cake.

And you know what really upsets me even more when I come to think about it? When I was lacing into him as he lay on the floor curled up in agony, it felt great. I was actually enjoying it!

XX

"Sunderland and proud, whatever the position,
in whatever the division!"

So how do you pick yourself up following such a massive let down? For me, and strangely enough, the semi–final game brought back a buzz that I'd missed for a long, long time. I felt I had gained back my fever pitch, my Mackem radicalism, and fervour for the game. With victory over Wimbledon a few days later, another three points in the forthcoming Good Friday match against Sheffield United would place us once more within catching distance of the top two, and although it was a game that was live on television, I had to go – my new found addiction demanded it.

The game itself was amazing. If a team had to pick itself up and carry as if nothing had happened, Sunderland AFC would be way down the list in my reckoning. And yet the way in which we played football, walking all over Sheffield United was astounding. Jason McAteer, the villain a week earlier played an excellent game – pity he didn't do that against Millwall. Goals from Tommy Smith, Gary Breen and right at the death, Kevin Kyle put Sunderland within five points of automatic promotion.

Scoring early eased the pre–match tension that was self–evident. After seven minutes Tommy Smith found the back of the net, a goal scored from a move initiated by him with a pass to McAteer on the right who skipped passed a few challenges before whipping in a cross for Smith to nod home at the near post. Gary Breen scored a headed goal from a Thornton corner in the middle period of the second half, and the rout was completed in the ninetieth minute when second half substitute Kevin Kyle slotted home.

McCarthy had got his tactics spot on for this one. With SAFC having a large squad, the manager, obviously influenced by Claudio Ranieri's Chelsea, had started to adopt his own

122

rotation system. This match had seven changes made to the starting eleven compared with the line-up from the midweek win over Wimbledon. Although many disagree with such drastic changes (I personally always take the view of, "If it ain't broke, don't fix it"), provided players are injury free, and no suspensions are put in place, then I, like many believe a manager should keep a winning side together. But who was I to argue at this moment in time? The Lads had shaken off the disappointment of the semi-final and had taken six valuable league points in the space of four days.

The win boosted the players, boosted the fans, and although only 27,000 turned out, it set-up a mouth watering and potential full house clash a week later against second placed West Bromwich Albion. Victory over Ipswich Town on Easter Monday could, if results went our way, put us just two points behind West Brom prior to the game kicking off.

Principally it meant that by keeping up the momentum of league victories, we would be back into the Premiership at the first attempt and although a cup final would've been a romantic encounter, being back in the top flight after only one year would be seen my many as essential. In the history of the Premiership less than a handful of clubs have bounced back at the first attempt. Sunderland had not managed that, but destiny was in our own hands and bouncing back was ever so near.

But we are cursed, remember. We are doomed to failure. Supporting SAFC appears to be more of a case of being disappointed than being ecstatic. Last time around, a defeat at Portman Road effectively ended our chances of automatic promotion and led us into 'that' play off final, and of course defeat (we're cursed I tell ya).

Portman Road is therefore a dangerous place for Sunderland and not always a happy hunting ground. However a 'shock' win in the fourth round of the F. A. Cup meant confidence would be installed in the players and their attitude would be one of, "We did it a few months back, we're on a run of five successive league wins, and even though Ipswich's form of late has been second to none, we can win".

Full time: Ipswich Town 1 Sunderland 0. A first half stoppage time penalty by Sunderland fan and former *'Monkey Hanger'* Tommy Miller put a major dent in our promotional aspirations. But we could still turn things around. We still had to play both West Bromwich Albion and Norwich City the Stadium of Light, which was now reverting back to being a fortress once again (we hadn't lost a game at home since September).

Come Sunday 18th April 2004, 32,201 brave souls watched a tough encounter (I was the one). Mick McCarthy made four changes to the team that lost at Portman Road. West Brom however had set out their stall to spoil our plans. They sat back and absorbed wave after wave of attacks. We tried. Fucking hell did we try! With a first half shut out, and an unfortunate early exit by George McCartney – stretchered–off after a tackle for a loose ball – Mick McCarthy threw on Kevin Kyle as a third striker as we desperately pushed further forward in search of a goal. Kyle almost scored with more or less his first touch. Carl Robinson – a midfielder on loan from Portsmouth looped a dangerous header towards goal, but the Baggies keeper saved. Minutes later Robinson fired in a half volley – wide. Arca shot wide, Oster failed to connect with a golden chance, a penalty shout was ignored by the referee following a dangerous cross from Gary Breen, and in the dying seconds Phil Babb connected with a cross from Tommy Smith only to see his header saved.

West Brom's stubborn defence wouldn't budge and any attack they managed to start normally ended up with an offside flag as our own defence stood strong. But as luck would have it, cue my favourite three word phrase – 'for fucks sake' – the Baggies snatched victory in the ninetieth minute.

Curses!

Well, that was it. As the final whistle was blown, automatic promotion was but a memory and a case of the *'if only's'* again – the toilet had been flushed and Sunderland were left standing watching a winning lottery ticket disappear *'down the pan'*.

So close and yet so far away. Five league wins had been sadly followed by two nasty 1–0 defeats. This deflated the team and deflated the fans. Of course it couldn't get any worse, could it? Three days later we travelled to Selhurst Park, or rather *'Hell hurt'* Park as it is affectionately known in certain circles. Personally I fucking hate that place. It has never been a ground to go to and enjoy a victory. The team had five changes made to it and lost 3–0, Mart Poom being sent off after less than thirty minutes. We were falling apart and if we weren't careful we could end up not even qualifying for the play-offs. Suddenly we were nose diving. We couldn't score. The rotation system, never mind forced changes, was now no longer working. McCarthy was becoming tactically inept. Yet he made four more changes as we travelled down to Wigan, a surprise package in the First Division, and a stubborn team that had dwelt in the top six for almost the entire season. A goalless draw meant we hadn't scored in almost six hours of football, and failure to grab all three points guaranteed promotion to West Brom. Our best bet was the Play-Offs, but at this rate, would we be able to remain in the top six? Our form was appalling. Other teams were breathing down our necks, Sheffield United, West Ham, Wigan, Crystal Palace, Ipswich Town. Only four would make it into the play-off's. Would we be one of them? Two home games would or could decide that one, the first a guaranteed three points against lowly Crewe Alexandra. But confidence was shot. McCarthy, with only one change looked to gel a team that although it hadn't scored at Wigan, had kept a clean sheet. We managed a goal from Jeff Whitley of all people, but it wasn't enough. As pressure mounted for us to get a second and kill off the game, Crewe struck and snatched a draw. It meant we were spilling dangerously close to a season promising so much, and yet ending with nothing. Three days later Norwich City arrived, hoping to be crowned champions, whilst for Sunderland, a win would secure a play-off position. Four changes were made, resulting in a 1–0 win courtesy of loan player Carl Robinson. Seven years on from a game voted one of the all–time greatest matches played at Wembley, we were in the lottery once again. What lay ahead were three games, two–hundred and seventy minutes of football between success, and an eleventh hour reprieve for Bob Murray and Co. Norwich were still crowned champions as West Brom playing at Stoke the same night, lost 4–1 and therefore handed the Canaries the crown.

We therefore had one more game, an away tie at Burnley, a game without pressure, and as such a 2–1 win. That put us third. Season over. We finished six points being West Bromwich Albion. Six fucking points! So fucking close! The play-offs beckoned. We were in third place, the so-called unlucky slot. We had a two-legged affair against Crystal Palace to overcome. We'd just played them and fallen apart, but we had claimed victory over the Eagles at home earlier in the season. This wasn't going to be easy. In my view, if we could get to the final we'd go up. There was no way fate would put us through another play-off final defeat. Crystal Palace wasn't going to be easy, but it was doable.

XXI

"No Excuses. I went to the match on my wedding day I did!"

The play-offs; the proverbial luck of the draw; a lottery; a heads or tales sudden death competition pitting the four teams to miss out on a top two position and automatic promotion into the riches of the promised land. We've been there before, on two occasions (I'm not going to dwell on the obvious third being the *'relegation play-offs'* that sent us into the old Division Three). Each time a final appearance was assured, but each time we fell at the last, the first an own goal by Gary *'Shiney'* Bennett against Swindon Town in 1990, though as we all know Swindon were renamed *'Swindle'* due to their *'swindling'* and we were granted promotion through the back door. The second time we lost in *'that'* game against Charlton.

So here we were again, on the brink of yet another final. Surely this time we wouldn't fuck up. We'd lost the last four times we'd appeared at Wembley. This time, with Cardiff's Millennium Stadium beckoning, we surely wouldn't screw it up. Likewise this was our second semi-final within a month. We'd lost to Millwall in the F. A. Cup, but with two legs we could without a shadow of a doubt defeat sixth placed Crystal Palace even though they had embarrassed us just a few weeks earlier. If we reached the final we'd go up. It was as simple as that. We'd never lost a play-off semi-final, the omens were good (but me being me, I had this awful feeling that we'd not be going to Cardiff).

With the first leg at *'Hell hurt'* Park, and with the recent 3-0 defeat still fresh in most Mackems' memories, I imagined those making the trip to London, as well as those anticipating watching the game on telly would be trying to work out what would be the most realistic result to hope for. Bearing in mind that away goals no longer counted, if we lost, then hopefully it would be by one goal and no more. We'd defeated Palace at home early in the season, the Stadium of Light was a fortress of late (if you exclude the West Brom defeat), so any loss in the first leg could be made up in the second. Well that's how my mind was working out the possible permutations.

In a tight first half SAFC, made a couple of half decent chances, and at the break were the happier of the two teams. Vociferous support from the usual high turn out of Mackems was a welcome sight and a welcome sound - at least we had more than one chant, all Palace appeared to be able to muster was the unvarying "Eee-gulls".

What struck me in the first period was Jason McAteer's commitment to the cause. He was up for it, but was unfortunately wearing his imbecilic head. Therefore, mirroring the performance in the F. A. Cup semi-final, the daft twat got himself booked for a stupid, niggling challenge - one of many he made in the first forty five minutes. What we didn't want was to be down to ten men at this early stage of the play-offs.

Mick McCarthy must have felt the same as Sean Thornton came on for the second half and for the *'neutral'* armchair fan a treat was in store. Sunderland, pressuring whenever they could, were awarded a well deserved penalty when Carl Robinson

127

was brought down, though why Palace's Tony Popovic wasn't sent off is beyond me. I'm not too au fait with the rules of the game, but I thought last man and all that meant instant red. Marcus Stewart (our top scorer) back in the team, coolly slotted home for SAFC. People appear to either love or despise Stewart for some reason. Admiration for the bloke appears to swing from one end of the scale to the other. Whichever side of the fence you stand on though, he can (at the time of writing) take penalties. The Mackem army in London cheered with joy. In Sunderland, cheers could be heard all around the City. In the pubs, beer was unashamedly split. In homes, beer was unashamedly spilt. I split my beer, though my daughter, having a sleepover party, was ashamed (she's at that age where Dad is but an embarrassment). By the time I'd wiped away the spillage, it was one all. Palace immediately attacked, and did so viciously and without remorse. Neil Shipperley looped home a header that Mart Poom could only watch in despair.

Luck, remember, had deserted the name of Sunderland Association Football Club a few years ago. The superstition of the lucky black cat had long since gone, and yet recently luck, it would appear, had been slowly returning. Let us not forget though, the title of this book. We are cursed, and in this game 'luck' swayed venomously towards Palace. Ten or so minutes later they went 2–1 up, courtesy of a bizarre deflection off Phil Babb – well it had to be Babb, the player blamed for the F. A. Cup defeat along with McAteer, Thirlwell, and a few others.

Kevin Kyle, though, wouldn't let it lie and towards the end of the game he appeared to have salvaged the tie. Suddenly we had levelled at two–all. Why didn't away goals count any more? Once again though, luck favoured the home side, and before you could say, "Fuck the Mags", Palace were 3–2 up – a shot that Poom should have held but quite simply couldn't hold.

The game however, and the result was marred by the 'over–celebrating' of the Palace 'fans' who on the final whistle invaded the pitch. On one hand, such sights are common occurrences, especially at an end of season bash. However on this occasion, with very few stewards or police visible, the invading fans headed straight towards the Sunderland contingent, and inevitably a *'Barney Rubble'* took place. From all accounts a Sunderland fan was stabbed either during this fracas or afterwards, the warm weather meant many supporters had taken off their tops and the non–scarfers unable to tell who was who started throwing punches at anyone and everyone, be it the Sunderland fans holding back from all out retaliation or their own fans – stupid cockney wankers.

Crystal Palace Football Club had fucked up here with their *'security'* measures. There was a distinct lack of any preparation to deal with such a scenario. But, this was just Crystal Palace and therefore no F A, or police investigation took place. If it had been Millwall or Chelsea, well I'm sure the headlines would have been of the front page variety. In my opinion someone somewhere did not take into account just how tense and emotional people get in games like these. So much is at stake that you have a tinder box ready to ignite at the slightest of moments. If you recall, the Palace fan I'd sat next too on my little stint at fame – "The Premiership's Greatest" television show – was anything but friendly. The actions of the encroaching home fans was of no real surprise to me, nor, come to think of it, was the amount of Burberry on show.

With Euro 2004 just around the corner, both legs of the play–off games were squashed together. Palace away took place on Friday 14th May. The return leg at the Stadium of Light took place a mere three days later on Monday 17th May. The play–off finals always take place over a bank holiday weekend, the Monday being the climatic First Division match. This time around the *'Premiership Final'* was to take place on the Saturday of the bank holiday weekend. It may have been only two days, but the F A were determined to get this *'big'* game out of the way as soon as possible so that their, and the nations focus would be on England's bid to become the "Champions of Europe", once Euro 2004 kicked–off in Portugal, and the sizeable contingent of Division One internationals (not English, obviously) reported for Euro 2004 in accordance with UEFA rules. It left little time to breath, get a ticket for the second leg (well for non–season ticket holders it was), as well as plan a possible day trip to Cardiff!

What surprised me about the return leg was the attendance. I went. Others who like me were still pissed at the Club went. But it would appear not enough of 'us' went. The official attendance was 34,536, with at least 2,000 being Palace fans. Either the Monday night kick–off was to blame, finances, the recent F. A. Cup semi final defeat, or the fact that we'd been relegated just twelve months previously, on top of Bob Murray still being the head honcho – one or any of these was probably why this game wasn't a sell–out. Whatever the reasons, the atmosphere didn't suffer. It was electric! Tensions, as expected, were once again high. We had to score to get back into the tie. If we won, and won by two goals, we'd be Cardiff bound. At half–time I had shit my pants. The scoreboard displayed, Sunderland 2 Crystal Palace 0. Fucking hell! We were going to do it! In my head I was trying to work out how I'd get to Cardiff, how much it would cost and thought about how many tickets I'd end up with, or whether or not to try to blag another press pass.

Here we were, forty–five minutes away from the play–off final, two goals in as many minutes, and in as many minutes before the break – Kyle on 43, Stewart on 45. Could you fucking believe it? I was sitting in the upper part of the North Stand with about five other people – really there was only about five people in the upper part of the North Stand – but like the thirty odd thousand below, anticipation was high, and gloom and doom was nigh!

Palace however refused to lie down and die. The spirit that manager Ian Dowie had instilled in the team since taking over merited great applause. From being there or thereabouts, struggling at the foot of the table when he took charge, the turnaround he had accomplished, taking them into the Play-Offs at the last minute was worthy of the accolades flying around. And much like that last gap dive into a play off position, a last gap goal took this tie into extra time. Down to ten men after Julian Gray was sent off for a reckless challenge on Jason McAteer in the 85th minute, you'd have all but written off the Eagles, five minutes left and one man short.

But you know what? When it comes to discussions about SAFC, there is always a *'but'*. On this occasion it wouldn't be any different, for on ninety-one minutes, a minute into the four minutes of allocated injury time, a corner swung in from Palace's Shaun Derry was met by substitute Darren Powell who headed in the leveller, past Poom, who with my red and white rose tinted glasses on was fouled (fast forward to the England V. Portugal Euro 2004 quarter-final and the Sol Campbell goal – that one was disallowed when there was nothing wrong with it, yet Palace's equaliser stood when there was blatantly something wrong with it).

Extra time meant both teams cautiously playing defensively and that meant the inevitable was inevitable. One of the biggest curses to befall SAFC was now yet again reality once more – the penalty shoot-out.

By now we had lost one definite and possibly one other first choice spot-kick taker. Marcus Stewart's penalty taking was during the 2003–2004 season second to none, but he had been substituted late in the game. Sean Thornton, a player with skill and talent, had also been taken off. Prior to the actual kicks being taken, I tried to work out who the five takers would actually be. But, I couldn't work I out. If a drop of luck remained in the SAFC camp, then I prayed that it would show itself now.

What was about to unfold before my eyes and thousands of others, was five kicks that could wipe Sunderland's debt in an instant, restore pride to the stay-aways, and (sadly) save Bob Murray's neck once again.

Sunderland won the toss.

Up stepped John Oster, who... missed (oh no).

Palace's Andrew Johnson stepped up, struck the ball ... 1–0 to the visitors.

Tommy Smith then marched up and scored (thank fuck for that). Dougie Freedman then scored for Palace. Phil Babb then headed towards the penalty spot and my heart sank. But he scored! Neil Shipperley then put Palace 3-2 up with a clean strike, before Carl Robinson made it 3-3.

Tony Popovic kept up Palace's one-hundred percent strike rate putting the fifth and potentially final kick for Sunderland in the hands of Gary Breen, but the potential player of the season, scored with ease.

It was now down to Crystal Palace's Shaun Derry. The ball was placed on the spot, he took a few steps back, took a deep breath, head down at first, before looking up at the goal, the towering figure of Mart Poom between him and a Cardiff final. He ran up; hit the ball and… Poom saved it.

Fucking get in!

All five penalties had been taken. Oster's miss was wiped out as 'The Poominator' saved the day.

Sudden death!

First up was Jason McAteer often the villain, occasionally the hero, and always the joker. This time he became the villain (again) as his spot kicked was saved by Palace keeper Nico Vaesen.

Fuck, Fuck, Fuck.

Piss, piss, piss.

Twat, twat, twat.

It was down to Poom again to keep us in this tie. Facing him was Wayne Routledge, and would you believe it, Poom saved it once again!

Yes!

This was now totally and utterly unbearable.

Then up stepped Jeff Whitely. Vasean saved a bad penalty from Whitely who for some bizarre reason thought he was Thierry Henry or something with his run up, hesitant stop, and strike that was completely and utterly bollockesed-up (I'm sure the racist element in the supporting ranks of SAFC enjoyed that one). Mart Poom was now on a hat-trick of saves, should he keep out the next strike taken by Michael Hughes.

Alas it was not to be.

Hughes scored.

I couldn't move, nor speak, nor even swear.

The game was over, 2–1 on the night to Sunderland, 4–4 overall in the tie, and 5–4 to Palace in the deciding penalty shoot out.

The Premiership, so near, was once again ever so far away. We had almost gotten there, and gotten there with a team that really wasn't up to scratch, especially for Premiership survival. That thought wasn't of concern at the time. Getting back up at any cost, and in any way, shape, or form, was what mattered.

But this was Palace's season; they went on to win the Play–Off Final by beating West Ham. If it's of any consolation we had been spared at least a twelve month pardon from having to visit *'Hell hurt'* Park.

I left the Stadium of Light alone, quiet, saddened, shaking my head constantly on the way home, slumping into bed like a spoilt brat whose toy had broken, or who wasn't allowed to stay up late 'cos it was a school night.

Football and heartache is a mathematical formula that ultimately spells out the name of Sunderland Association Football Club.

I was disillusioned and pissed off again. It doesn't get any better does it? There appears to be no end in sight to this living nightmare we suffering fans of Sunderland AFC are currently enduring (and some would say have been doing so for over sixty odd years). We are cursed!

XXII

"An honest politician is one who,
when he is bought, will stay bought!"

Penalty shoot–outs, don't you just love them? If it's not SAFC, then it's our national squad. Step forward the shenanigans of Euro 2004. Initially, and as usual, hopes were high. Wayne Rooney was unveiled to a world wide audience of billions.

Suddenly the word *'Charva'* was being muted across the globe. Michael Owen was getting stick for not scoring. Once again everyone wondered why Emile Heskey was in the squad, and *'Captain Marvel'* himself, Mr. David *'Golden–balls'* Beckham was below par. I wonder though, how much his publicised shagging antics that the media kept hounding him with affected his game? As usual in any major footballing tournament England always crash out in controversial style. If it's not a bizarre goalkeeping error, or last minute panicking, it'll be a good old penalty shoot out that sends the national squad packing. We never get beat 3–0 or anything along those lines.

Against the Portuguese a repeat scenario of Sol Campbell thinking he'd scored the winner (versus Argentina in '98) only for a dodgy ref to disallow a perfectly good goal arose. And then, up stepped Michael Gray or rather David Beckham, catching a mole that had popped its head out of the sandpit being used as the penalty spot, before Darius Vassell became the David Batty, or Gareth Southgate, Chris Waddle, or closer to home the aforementioned Michael Gray, or Jason McAteer, or Jeff Whitley penalty taker heartbreaker.

Thankfully, if you can actually say such a thing, being a Sunderland supporter prepares you for such defeats, so the European Championships weren't too much of a disappointment. As the chant goes, "Are you Sunderland in disguise?"

On a personal note, towards the end of the season, I started to feel extremely good about myself. I'd recaptured my long lost lust for football, and had recently thrown the last of my prescription drugs in the bin. I'd been on anti–depressants for almost two years and if anything they were simply making me fat, unhealthy, and bad tempered. A few weeks of cold turkey later I started to lose weight, my temper eased considerably and recent pains in my chest had also subsided. It proved to me that, if you want to do something or achieve something, you have to do it yourself. In my opinion, my doctor had just kept on signing prescription after prescription, instead of encouraging me to come off these hard–core chemicals that were no longer effective and were now causing physical side–

effects. I guess it shows just how overworked doctors are, having to tend to far more patients on their panel than they can handle. You are no longer a face, but a number. Without any notes, they don't remember you and at times even with their notes they still don't know you. Therefore, I have to stress just how proud I am that I managed to free myself from such an addictive, and in recent times totally useless drug. In the early days, yes, they helped, as my health was without doubt extremely bad (though I often look back on those dark days and kid myself that it never happened).

Now even though I'm personally back on track, I still have issues. We all have. I still wait to piss on the grave of the person who worked for the company from Burnley who ripped off RTG. I never mentioned who by name in *Why Do I Do It?* and although in a draft version of this chapter I did and ripped into them without remorse, I've held back as believe it or not at the time of writing you could say that negotiations are underway to try and come to some sort of closure on all of this and its only taken three years to get to this point.

That's about as much as I'll say at the moment. However I have to draw your attention to Koptalk, the Liverpool FC version of Ready To Go, a site whose webmaster/dragon slayer emailed me shortly after the release of *Why Do I Do It?* to tell me that he too was also part of the aforementioned yet unmentioned organisation from Burnley and that he too had fallen into the same problems that RTG had. He took legal action and as he had some spare change to force through a court case, won, and proceeded to tell me how he bought a car for his mam with the money he had been awarded in damages or whatever the correct legal term is.

I wasn't particularly interested in someone telling me, "I won, you didn't nah, nah, nah, I got awarded a shit load of cash, and you did not".

But putting away such childish jealousy, I returned his email asking if he would supply the name of his solicitor as I was interested in contacting him and resurrecting RTG's case after all he'd be quite familiar with what had happened, and having won the case for Koptalk would probably be able to help out RTG.

I'm still waiting for him to get back to me and this is what pisses me off. Far too many people want to fucking brag about how clever they are and when you ask for a little bit of help (in this case just the name of a firm of lawyers) they ignore your plea. It's just so fucking annoying. It's not that I want to buy my mam a car; after all we're still *'estranged'* – to put it politely. She is no longer part of my life.

My parents are now officially divorced. I've not had any contact with my mother for almost a year, I no longer know where she lives and at this moment in time, I no longer care. I've just got my own shit back together and that is all that concerns me at present.

Moving on though, I have to write a sentence or two about how quickly SAFC made moves to please the masses of disappointed fans following the end of the season and the heartache of the playoffs, by removing a large chunk of dead wood from the playing staff with brutal ruthlessness. We often chant, "Bye, bye, bye, bye, bye, bye, bye, bye," to the tune of the Westminster Chime towards a red carded opposition player but following SAFC's quick thinking, it applied to the following players:

Paul *'The Crab'* Thirlwell,
Phil *'Own Goal'* Babb,
Tommy *'Inconsistent'* Smith,
Darren *'I'm Not Kevin Phillips'* Byfield,
Jason *'The Mouth'* McAteer,
Joachim *'Bought After His Sell Buy Date'* Bjorklund.

Now I've referred to McAteer as *'The Mouth'* which may appear too polite as I could've used words like arsehole, tosser, prick, dick, wanker, and so on. *'The Mouth'* arose in my mind from two things he said. First off he allegedly mouthed about Bob Murray needing to spend money as he needed to play around quality players. Now I'm not sticking up for Uncle Bob here, but McAteer needing quality to play with him – meaning exactly what – he isn't quality or thinks he is pure quality? Secondly I was slightly perturbed to read McAteer saying something along the lines of how losing in the Play–Offs was like mourning the death of someone. That to me stank of Neanderthal, speak first, brain kick in later dialogue (I know Neanderthal's couldn't speak, I'm just using the *'thick'* angle here to make my case).

During half time in the home leg, someone collapsed and died from a heart attack. McAteer's comments in the local newspaper came across a bit insensitive if you ask me. My attempts at contacting the press to point this out fell on dead ears (I wonder if the bloke who runs Koptalk, also runs the local papers web site).

Other players were also *'kicked–out'*, and one or two were borderline due to their contracts being up for renewal. Within a few weeks we'd signed a number of new faces, wingers, defenders, midfielders, and at the time of writing this, the look and feel of the squad was very promising.

With August looming (or by the time you read this, will have come and gone), it's a case of fingers crossed, and here we go again.

XXIII

"That which does not kill me, postpones the inevitable!"

So, to sum up everything! Well, the best way I can conclude what all this waffle is actually about is by owning up to being cursed. Yes, that's right, I am cursed. Why? Well, I'm cursed due to an unhealthy obsession towards my football club. I'm cursed because I care about SAFC. I want them to be in the Premiership on a permanent basis. I want us winning things. I want us to be, by far the greatest team the world has ever seen. I want victory, glory, satisfaction. I want the Mags to be relegated. I want to be happy.

But I'm cursed. All of us are cursed. We're born on this corrupt planet of ours, born into what can only be described, with a little philosophical thinking – hell and we are made to suffer.

My first venture into the world of red and white euphoria stems back to a dark, cold, and wet mid–week game at Roker Park, against Nottingham Forest. We lost 3-2 (surprise, surprise). That was the start of my *'road trip'* and it didn't get any better. Wembley '85 and defeat, St. James Park New Years Day '85, and a *'racist'* defeat, '86 and Beelzebub himself took over – McMenemy – and two years of pain ended with Division Three football. This curse was lifted by instant promotion, and the spawning of the *'G-Force'*, the '90 play-off semi–final success, and promotion into the top flight via the back door, much to the dismay of the black and white heathen scum.

Luck however appears to run out far too quickly for SAFC and after one year, a last match defeat at Maine Road – heartache sets in and the curse returns. Queue the dark, dark days of limbo, Crosby, Buxton, Butcher, though the clouds briefly lift in '92 with an F. A. Cup final, one that was full of hope, but delivered defeat. *'The Don'* came and went, and then in a moment of madness, or sheer desperation, our beloved chairman asks Peter Reid to step in and save us from another relegation bound nightmare.

He does!

The clouds part once more, only this time blue skies shine down on Roker Park. Queue a championship–winning team and promotion for the first time into the Premiership.

But we're cursed remember and, after just one season, we were back to square one. The fans are now bickering with each other, split over leaving Roker Park and moving to The Stadium Of Light. That however is the signal to start a season full of excitement – the birth of Super-Kev!

But we're cursed.

We end up astray in London, the play-offs being once more oh so cruel.

And then an anomaly!

Something went wrong because everything from August 1998 to August 2001 went right.

We were promoted in a season beyond belief.

We scored back-to-back, 2-1 wins against the Skunks in their own backyard.

We had two successive seventh placed finishes.

The cursed was lifted!

Or was it?

Actually it was taunting us, playing with us, fucking with our minds and our sense of well being. We had three glorious and unbelievable seasons and that meant punishment. A mediocre last day grace was followed by the worse relegation in the history of the Premiership.

We were back to square one.

Peter Reid was now a hated figure.

Bob Murray? Well I can't put into print what I think of Bob Murray!

Super-Kev was but a distant memory. Niall Quinn had long since retired. The sexy 4-4-2 formations of talented wingers – Johnston and Summerbee were no more.

We had lost all hope.

Disillusionment was rife.

Hope and fulfilment had deserted a sunken ship!

The team and the Club were quickly and affordably re-built. It tried to grab back glory with immediate effect and it came close – two semi-finals – but that of course means nothing.

We are cursed!

Is there any hope for us?

Well, yes there is, but we must first just accept that shit happens. Unfortunately for SAFC supporters, it happens far too often. Whatever smooth and enjoyable times we have, for some reason we appear to have to suffer the rough, and it hurts – skin raw, bleeding wounds – physical and psychological torture.

When you come to think about it though, it could be worse. The Mags might have actually reached the UEFA Cup Final and won the bloody thing. I know the Smoggies won the League

Cup, but thankfully they are just a small town in Yorkshire and the residents of Wearside don't give a shit about those who dwell in and around Teesside.

However what if the Mags had won the UEFA Cup, how would you feel? Would it be a case of, "Well they mean nothing to me, if it's not Sunderland why should it bother me?" Or would it be, "Fucking black and white bastards?" Or, as many point out, would it be, "Congratulations Newcastle well done, after if we had won such a competition I'm sure they would return the compliments?" Could we as Sunderland fans live with Newcastle actually winning things while we struggle in a lower league? Would calls for Bob Murray's head bring results? Sometimes I think the only way our chairman will leave is if Newcastle actually do win something. At that moment most Sunderland fans would be so jealous and pissed off that Murray would face a mutiny unlike anything any other club will have witnessed in the history of Association Football. Maybe then, what Sunderland need to move on is for Newcastle to win something? Yes I'm waving a banner that reads *'Murray Out'*, and yes for making such as stance critics will turn around and say if Murray leaves then who exactly would take over? I can't answer that, who knows who would be brave enough to take over, but someone would, just because nobody is publicly making suggestions that they want overall control doesn't necessarily mean that there is no one out there. I personally can't be arsed with the *better the devil you know* scenario. I want Murray to leave as he has caused far too much damage and made too many fans despise him for steering SAFC into the lowly position they find themselves in at present. Such tortuous moments in our recent history under the command of Mr. Murray far outweighs any successes we've had. I'll rephrase that, as we haven't had any successes. We've had good fortune, and memorable moments to cherish, winning the odd game here and there. We've had a new stadium built but that's about it really. So part of me has to say come on the Mags win something so we can be finally rid of a man who has guided us almost to the brink of oblivion.

However, we all know the Mags will win fuck all; their smugness prior to the UEFA cup semis was wiped away when they failed to progress into the final. We may be cursed, but if we had just reached a European Cup semi–final, and had just missed out on a Champions League spot, but had re–qualified for the UEFA Cup, would you at the last home game of the season, boo off your team or leave the ground and snub your club's lap of honour? How many SAFC supporters given such circumstances would? I know how many, it's obvious how many – none. We may be fickle, fuck knows I am, but should Sunderland ever reach the heights the Mags through sheer luck have, we the fans of SAFC would not boo or diss our Club in such a way. The Mags did, the sad bastards. After a 1-1 draw against relegated Wolverhampton Wanderers, the so–called supporters of Newcastle United Football Club left early, booed loudly, their manager – Sir Bobby *'Pissy Pants'* Robson was caught out having a dig at the very people who pay his wages, and less than 10,000 remained to bother with the end of season parade. Those 10,000 are the only *'true'* fans NUFC have – probably the same ones who averaged the Mags home gate prior to the Keegan era and the annoying and unbelievable fortuity they've managed to sustain since. SAFC now averages 26,000 and that's in a division lower and a team that is below par, under–performing, and has yet to show its true potential (again).

SAFC fans may be cursed, but we will at some point win something. The Mags however are thankfully doomed to the fact that they will never win anything. That is something we suffering Mackems can relish and it sidetracks the issue of being cursed.

So even though we are cursed, we can but continue to support. Remember, a fan blows hot and cold, but a supporter supports.

We love SAFC. We do.

Wise men say only fools rush in. Well, we must all be fools for we can't help but fall in love with SAFC. It is after all, a love supreme and yet as always, it's the hope we can't stand.

And so if being cursed is something if we cannot shake, we should then stare back at it with determination and embrace it, for it means no one season will ever be, nor has ever been the same. There is never a dull moment supporting SAFC.

Well, seeing as we did have a decent cup run during the 2003–2004 season, I have to be true to my word right? So as stated in the first chapter of this book,

"I love Alan Shearer!"